TE

2016

D0343967

90710 000 267 371

EX LIBRIS

It's All Going Wonderfully Well

ROSA HOSKINS
AND RICHARD BUTCHINS

HUTCHINSON
LONDON

1 3 5 7 9 10 8 6 4 2

Hutchinson
20 Vauxhall Bridge Road
London SW1V 2SA

Hutchinson is part of the Penguin Random House group of companies
whose addresses can be found at global.penguinrandomhouse.com.

Penguin
Random House
UK

Copyright © Rosa Hoskins and Richard Butchins 2016

Rosa Hoskins has asserted her right to be identified as the author of this
Work in accordance with the Copyright, Designs and Patents Act 1988.

Lines from 'The Beautiful Frock' by Edward Monkton reprinted by kind
permission from Edward Monkton.

Picture credits: **5** © Photos 12/Alamy Stock Photo; **6** © The Ronald Grant Archive;
15 Herbie Knott/Shuttershock; **16** © AF archive/Alamy Stock Photo. All other
photos courtesy of the author.

First published in the UK by Hutchinson in 2016

www.penguin.co.uk

A CIP catalogue record for this book is available from the British Library.

ISBN 9780091959074 (hardback)

Typeset in 11.75 /18.25 pt Bell MT Std
Jouve (UK), Milton Keynes
Printed and bound in Great Britain by Clays Ltd, St Ives Plc

MIX
Paper from
responsible sources
FSC® C016897

Penguin Random House is committed to a
sustainable future for our business, our readers
and our planet. This book is made from Forest
Stewardship Council® certified paper.

For my family

London Borough of Richmond Upon Thames		
RTTE		
90710 000 267 371		
Askews & Holts		
B HOS		£14.99
		9780091959074

AUTHOR'S NOTE

My DAD NEVER LET the truth get in the way of a good story. His stories would be embellished and exaggerated with each telling, often merging with other stories until they became one magnificent tale. I've investigated the origins of his anecdotes with people who were actually there, and sometimes they contradict Dad's version of events. However, there are some fanciful yarns that I'd always assumed were nonsense, but while going through Dad's old stuff I'd find cold, hard evidence that a story was in fact true and just as Dad had described it.

One of his favourites was about auditioning for a repertory company, early on in his career. He sat in the auditorium, waiting his turn, when suddenly a brouhaha erupted from backstage. The leading actress of the company came running on stage left, in floods of tears. Hot on her trail was the leading man, who grabbed her by the shoulder, turned her around and then punched her square in the face.

She crumpled and passed out on the floor. Realising that an auditorium full of people had just witnessed him strike a woman, the actor dashed off stage right. Seconds later, a dumpy stage manageress bounced on to the stage, looked at the concussed woman prostrate on the floor, and addressed the assembled actors in a high-pitched warble:

'It's all going wonderfully well!'

This story went down in the annals of our family history, and Dad trotted the phrase out at every minor catastrophe. When his car broke down on a deserted country road. The time I fell down the stairs during a party, aged thirteen, in front of forty guests. Or the year when one of the Christmas decorations caught fire. His humour was arch and irreverent. His comic timing was pinpoint precise and could cut through the tension of any mishap.

This book has been written as a tribute to my dad, and even though it's often been a painful experience, I'm glad I've recorded our relationship. When eventually I have children, I'll give them this and they'll know who their granddad was. I'll think of him every day for the rest of my life, and I'm forever grateful that he was mine.

PROLOGUE

YESTERDAY MY DAD WAS moved into the intensive care unit at the Princess Grace Hospital. For the past three weeks, he's been receiving treatment for an acute chest infection that his helpless body, ravaged by an aggressive degenerative disease, can no longer fight. His condition is critical. He doesn't have long.

The ICU is bright and noisy. It makes the soulless beige room he was in before seem cosy. Walking to Dad's section is disorientating: the sound of his rattling breath echoes down the corridor. I arrive at his room and greet him with my usual forced cheer.

'Hiya, Dad. How are you today?'

'Very well.'

His stoicism is unbreakable. Throughout his three-year illness, he has been strong for us – my mum Linda, my younger brother Jack, and Alex and Sarah, Dad's two children from his first marriage. He has never agonised about himself or the terrible void he is facing. His main concern has been how his illness was affecting my mum.

Keeping vigil over the dying is an exhausting ordeal because, for the most part, there's nothing that can be done. During the past few weeks, my mum and I have spent every day in the hospital with him. Watching as he gradually slips away from us has been a slow torture.

Mum has gone out to get a change of scene for a couple of hours. This place is oppressive, and we each take a break during the day.

From the ICU window there's a view of Baker Street. I can see the queue for Madame Tussauds snaking down the pavement.

'Why do so many tourists go to Madame Tussauds?' I wonder out loud. 'Do you remember the model they made of you, Dad?'

I stand in his eye line. He has an oxygen mask strapped across his face. His breath is ragged and his skin is red and clammy. He's surrounded by beeping machines and he has a drip in his arm.

His eyes flicker with recognition. His wax effigy stood in Tussauds years ago. It didn't look much like him – more like a disgruntled cousin.

I push a wheeled office chair across his room and manage to smash it into a bank of expensive medical equipment. After clobbering the machines that are keeping him alive, I sit down next to him. I try to adjust the height of his bed and press the wrong button. He judders up and down like a stuttering forklift.

Dad looks at me from above his condensation-filled face mask. Beneath it, I can see a flash of his old sardonic grin.

'Got any more winners for us?' he croaks.

CHAPTER ONE

I AWAKE FOR THE first time in a world without Dad. I stumble out of bed, take a shower and attempt to munch on some toast, but breakfast is a lost cause. All food tastes like sand. On the short walk to my parents' house – a few doors down from my own – a friend calls my mobile.

He is crying. 'I'm so sorry, darling. I just feel so sad for you all.'

I finish the conversation and ring Mum's doorbell.

We slump at the kitchen table and drink cups of tea. I drink mine out of a cup emblazoned with the letter B. We are shocked and bewildered. Even though we knew he was going to die, the reality that he's finally gone is stunning. We've spent the past couple of months in hospital, by his side, and we've become institutionalised.

When someone dies, there are copious amounts of grim administration to be carried out. Phone calls have to be made, the death itself registered, and funeral arrangements set in motion. The first thing we do is compile a list of people who we want to tell before the news breaks. We split the list in two and set about the business of calling our friends and family.

Reactions vary, from the calm acceptance of the people who have known that the end was imminent, to shocked tears from those who were unaware of the seriousness of Dad's condition. I do my best to give them the news with composure, but often I dissolve into tears myself.

I make my last call and go to sit with Mum in the kitchen. Dad's coat and hat still hang on the coat hook in the hallway. As I pass them, I stop and drink in a deep breath: they still smell of him.

Mum calls Dad's agent, who will later put out a press release. We go back to my house, where Alex, Sarah, Jack and my husband, Pete, are up. Pete busies around, making sandwiches and endless cups of tea.

The news breaks at lunchtime. Dad's agent calls to tell us it's on the TV. We stare at the lifeless box, not daring to turn it on. After a few minutes I grab the remote, the telly jabbers into life and I turn it over to the BBC News Channel. Sure enough, Dad's face is plastered all over the screen and presenters are relaying the news that Bob Hoskins has died after a bout of pneumonia. They read the statement that has been delivered by Dad's agent: 'We are devastated by the loss of our beloved Bob. We ask that you respect our privacy during this time and thank you for your messages of love and support.'

We watch the news spin around for a few minutes and then we switch it off. Silence briefly descends on the kitchen before our phones start to beep and buzz. A couple of journalists call to ask if I wish to make a comment. How they got hold of my number I will never know.

One female journalist sounds a touch embarrassed. 'I'm terribly sorry for your loss,' says the quavering voice, 'and I'm sorry to disturb you, but would you like to pay tribute to your dad?'

'No.'

'OK. Again, I'm sorry to disturb you and I'm sorry for your loss.'

'If you were that sorry for my loss, you wouldn't disturb me,' I say and hang up.

It is the sort of thing Dad would have said. Once, when Francis Ford Coppola offered him a part in *The Cotton Club*, he phoned our house at midnight.

'Hi,' said a voice. 'This is Francis Ford Coppola.'

'Yeah!?' said Dad. 'And this is Henry the Eighth — you've just woken up my kid!'

The call prompts me to think how I would like to pay tribute to my dad. Over the last week, I've written a list of the advice that Dad gave to me over the years. I was anxious that my already-frayed memory would unravel entirely and his words would slip away from me. One sunny afternoon, as I sat by his bed with light from the window streaming over my shoulder, his voice rang in my head as clear as a bell and I frantically jabbed away at the screen of my phone, recording his words.

I decide to publish Dad's advice – '11 Lessons from my Dad' – on my blog, Haute Hoskins. It's a fashion blog, which I launched a few years ago. I started my career as a jobbing actress, but I found the constant rejection and insecurity drove me to distraction. I never wanted to give up on acting – I rarely give up on anything – but I decided to try to find a day job that I enjoyed and started out as a personal stylist. That led to a job at an online magazine, which in turn led to me writing a blog. This in turn spawned other writing projects. Over the years, it has begun to gain in popularity and I have a decent following.

Here are the '11 Lessons':

My darling dad has died. I loved him to the ends of the earth and he loved me back just the same. These are the lessons he taught me; I will keep them close to my heart and remind myself of them whenever I stumble and falter. They are his words; the words spoken so often to encourage, comfort and reassure. This isn't general wisdom, rather advice that he tailor-made just for me. I love you, Dad.

1. Laugh. There's humour to be found everywhere; even in your darkest days there's something to have a

joke about. Laugh long and loud and make other people laugh. It's good for you.

2. Be yourself. If someone doesn't like you, they're either stupid, blind or they've got bad taste. Accept who you are; you've got no one else to be. Don't try to change yourself; there's no point. Don't apologise. Don't make excuses. Be yourself and if anyone else doesn't like it, they can fuck off.

3. Be flamboyant. It's who you are and always have been. Be eccentric and unique. Don't try to adapt yourself to someone else's view of normal. That belongs to them, not you. Like yourself as you are.

4. Don't worry about other people's opinions. Everyone's a critic but ultimately what they say only matters if you let it. Don't believe your own press. People can just as easily sing your praises as they can tear you down. Don't waste your time on things you can't change. Let it slide off you like water off a duck's back.

5. Get angry. It's OK to lose your temper now and then. If anger stays in, it turns to poison and makes you bitter and sad. Get angry, say your piece, then let it go.

6. Whatever you do, always give it a good go. Don't be afraid of failure and disappointment. If you fall flat on your face, then get straight back up. You'll always regret not trying. Disappointment is temporary, regret is for ever.

7. Be generous and kind because you can't take it with you. When you've got something to give, give it without hesitation.

8. Appreciate beauty. Take pictures and make memories. Capture it. You never know when it will be gone.

9. Don't take yourself too seriously. People who take themselves too seriously are boring.

10. Never, ever, ever, ever give up. Keep on punching, no matter what you're up against. You're only defeated if you give up. So don't give up.

11. Love with all your heart. In the end, love is the only thing that matters.

What happens next is a surprise. Alex and Sarah leave – they're as shell-shocked as the rest of us and they want the comfort of home – and Mum and I go for a walk in the local woods. We trudge around looking at the freshly sprouted leaves and flowers. All I can think is that Dad is not in the world any more. It's unfathomable. With every step, my phone vibrates in my pocket. My tribute to Dad has gone viral.

I suppose the '11 Lessons' confirms the public's perception that my dad was a good man, the kind of person they would want to call a friend. All my life I've had to share him with people who didn't really know him, people who would come up to him in the street and strike up a conversation as though they'd known him for ever.

I remember one time when he was in Waitrose in Lewes – we had a country house nearby. Dad was in the tea aisle, stocking up. (We Hoskinses drink vast quantities of the stuff.) A woman came up to him and said, 'Hey, Bob, where's the tea?'

He responded, 'Right in front of you, love.'

'No, that's all the herbal, fancy nonsense. Where's the *tea* tea?'

Dad helped her pick a box of PG Tips; the woman thanked him and went on her way.

Dad's public persona was different from how he was in private, as one might expect. But he possessed a down-to-earth likeability that was consistent whether he was in the supermarket or at a film premiere. I suppose that's why people related to him, and why the blog post has spread like wildfire.

In the City of Westminster Registrar's Office on the Harrow Road, Mum and I wait to register Dad's death. We sit in a waiting room with the other bereaved – hollow-eyed and grey-faced like us, a stark contrast to the new parents ferrying in their fresh babies to be checked into the system.

After we have waited what feels like for ever, a stout, jovial, middle-aged lady ushers us into a cramped office. She takes Dad's name, date of birth and date of death. She realises that Robert William Hoskins is actually Bob Hoskins and she nods, with a look of considered understanding.

'He was a popular man,' she says. 'I'm sure you'll miss him.'

It's a curious thing to say, but I suppose she has to say something.

I like the Jewish tradition of sitting shiva: for seven days after the funeral of a loved one, the immediate family stay in the home of the departed and other family and friends come to pay their respects and support the mourners. I suppose we have our own, non-religious version of shiva after Dad has died: friends come by, bringing flowers and food. It doesn't take away the pain, but it eases those first few days.

When I wake up in the mornings, I sometimes forget he's dead and feel OK for a brief moment. Then my dawning consciousness reminds me he's gone. It's like losing him all over again.

There is considerable outside pressure to make Dad's funeral a showbiz event, studded with celebrities. But we know that if Dad were to plan his own funeral it would be an intimate affair with good friends and family. The idea of having a

Hello! magazine wake would have made Dad sick to his stomach. I can hear his voice in my head saying 'Fuck that!'

In accordance with Dad's unequivocal wishes, we plan a simple ceremony where the speakers are to be people who represent different parts of his life. His oldest friends, Dave Hill and Jane Wood, a married couple who Dad met on his second acting job, will pay tribute to his early years in the theatre. Jim Hart, who wrote the screenplay for the film *Hook*, will talk about the later, Hollywood years.

Music is a harder decision. Dad loved music; his taste was wide and eclectic. When I lived at home with my parents, he would frequently burst through the door brandishing a CD, insisting that I listen to it there and then.

We refer to his episode of *Desert Island Discs*, which was recorded back in the 1980s. This is a useful guide, but hearing Dad's voice when he was well, full of bustling energy and enthusiasm, is painful. Mum and I choose 'Bad Penny Blues' by Humphrey Lyttelton for the end of the ceremony. The jazz track has something of his offbeat humour.

I want to sing something. I know it will be a massive undertaking, standing just inches away from his coffin, but I feel compelled to do so. In the latter stages of Dad's illness, there were times when I hadn't known what to do to comfort him. He was sometimes so unresponsive and it was difficult to know what he needed. He had always enjoyed my singing, so I sang to provide us both with a little solace – his favourite songs by Nat King Cole, Gregory Porter, Bob Dylan. He did tell me to shut up every now and again, but generally I think it was comforting for him to hear my voice.

His illness caused him to forget that I could sing. One time when we were at home and I sang he exclaimed, 'You have a gift! Does your mother know?'

But what to sing?

I consider 'When I See an Elephant Fly' from *Dumbo*. *Dumbo* was one of Dad's favourite films – he was nothing if not unpredictable. I remember him singing his heart out to the song as we watched the film together when I was a kid. He had an uninhibited, childish exuberance. He was never bothered with appearing cool; that self-consciousness that comes with it would have stifled his sense of fun. 'When I See an Elephant Fly' sums up his *joie de vivre*.

But it doesn't seem quite right.

In Dad's final moments, as he took his last breaths, I sang 'Wolfcry' by Gregory Porter. This song feels right. I know it will be hard, but it is my way of saying that my dad raised a strong woman. My friend Margo Buchannan, who is a brilliant singer, agrees to rehearse with me and gives me some advice.

'Before you get up there,' she says, 'put all your feelings in a little box and give that box to me. I'll look after it for you and give it back when you've finished.'

Sometimes the compassion and emotional generosity of people astounds me.

The day of the funeral comes and I wake to glorious spring sunshine. I'm briefly reminded of my wedding day and half expect Dad to be downstairs with a mug of tea. I have a shower and carefully apply make-up; these rituals provide me with courage and solace. I've always had a tendency to dress up: putting on make-up and dressing in nice clothes gives me strength.

At my parents' house, my mother greets and entertains guests. I take myself upstairs to warm up my voice. I go into the room where Mum stores all of Dad's clothes: beautiful tailor-made suits, jeans, old denim shirts, jackets and coats.

I'm reminded of one of Dad's favourite stories from when we lived in New York while he was filming *The Cotton Club*. Out clothes-shopping one day, he went into Saks Fifth Avenue and made his way to the men's suit department.

He asked a snooty-looking shop assistant, 'Hello, mate, have you got anything in here for me?'

The camp young man looked Dad up and down and said, 'Oh honey, you gotta be kidding.'

Dad was thick-skinned and always saw the funny side – especially if he was the punchline.

An array of statues and artwork that Dad picked up on his

global travels are scattered around the room: Inuit, African, European, Native American and New Zealand tribal and religious artefacts line the shelves. It's a varied collection but they all have a common theme: each is stocky, solid and hewn from either stone or darkest mahogany.

After I'm satisfied that my voice is warmed up I go downstairs, just as the hearse draws up outside. I step out and look at the coffin, covered in white flowers. I press my finger to the window of the car. The emotions that have been safely stowed away burst out in a small explosion. I choke them back again.

We climb into cars and follow Dad at a slow, gentle pace. I sit next to Mum, holding her hand. She stares at the back of the hearse as if she's trying to make eye contact with Dad. She wants him to know that she's still with him.

We arrive at the crematorium and the pallbearers slide the coffin out from the hearse and cautiously heave it on to their shoulders. I wonder what would happen if someone lost their grip and the thing came crashing down, with the body spilling out of the casket. Has that ever happened? Is there a procedure for that sort of mishap?

My grim reverie is broken by my mother-in-law, Sandra. She takes my hand and says, 'You can do this.'

We prepare to walk down the aisle of the crematorium behind Dad. 'The Lark Ascending' by Vaughan Williams sings out. I'm suddenly struck by an image of Dad when he was young. We take our places at the front amidst the muffled tears and sniffs of the congregation.

All too quickly it's my turn to sing. I walk on to the stage and everything seems to vanish. The opening chords play and I'm transported back to the stuffy hospital room, consoling Dad in his final hours. Only this time I can sing properly, loud and clear. Every note, every word is for him.

The ceremony ends with 'Bad Penny Blues' and we file past the coffin, touching it and saying goodbye. It still isn't time to let go; there are people to meet and greet.

I've often thought the way we grieve in the West is repressed. We keep the real, heart-cracking grief muffled and out of public view. I admire cultures where the funeral is a time to weep and wail, where public grief is seen as a necessary part of the process. As is the custom in England, we all keep our sadness private during the day.

We smile and thank all the guests for coming.

At the wake, in a light and airy restaurant in Hampstead, everyone shares their memories of Dad: funny stories, his generosity, his wildness and his talent. There is a lot of laughter and warmth. I try to speak to everyone there. It's odd how adrenalin can facilitate strength: the fact that I'm standing upright and making polite conversation is absurd.

After speaking to many people I find Jean Que, one of Dad's cousins. She's a couple of years older than Dad and I'm struck by how similar Jean is to my late grandmother Elsie. She has the same calm timbre to her voice, the warm but assertive persona. Her down-to-earth honesty is settling. I find people who don't say what they actually mean difficult. It's one of the qualities I miss most about Dad.

After hours of strapping on a brave face, I am desperate to get home and finally let go of the pain.

Shortly after he was diagnosed in 2011, I attempted to write Dad's story. When someone loses their memory, they lose a vital part of themselves. We really are nothing more than our memories. I suppose I thought that I could somehow preserve an essence of my dad by recounting the experiences that formed him. I felt I would be able to connect the dots of his life and keep him whole. Even after he fell apart.

Dad was very supportive of the idea. In years gone by, he would probably have become overexcited (a Hoskins tendency). I started out on a scrabbling race to salvage his memories before a shroud descended over his ability to recall them. We set up camp in the living room of my parents' house, cups of tea and digestive biscuits to hand, and I recorded our conversations on my phone.

A few months into the project, I cracked. I had collected the family archive and spread photos, newspaper cuttings and awards across a desk. I tried to make sense of it all, but it was impossible. Enveloping myself in his past glory while he struggled to remember what had happened earlier that same day was unbearable. The contrast was stark and merciless.

As I listen back to the recordings I realise it was an uphill battle, and there is more silence than there are words. As is often the case with neurologically degenerative disorders, his long-term memory was reasonably intact – it was more recent events that evaporated.

I'm still furious with myself for not finishing those recordings. But I never quite gave up on the idea. I'm like my dad in that way: too stubborn to ever surrender. Once I start on something, I'm compelled to finish.

Ten days after the funeral I sit down to start work on a book about Dad. I start by mapping out his life, from when he was born in 1942 to the seminal roles that defined his career; when he met my mum in 1981 and our family life began; and when he became ill and died just over thirty years later. I realise the first person I need to speak to is Cousin Jean, as she and Dad spent time together when they were children. It's a daunting task; every word is painful. But just as I felt compelled to sing at his funeral, I want to pay tribute to my dad. It's my way of preserving his memory and creating a record that I can one day show my children.

CHAPTER TWO

IN AUTUMN 1942 A heavily pregnant Elsie Hoskins was evacuated from war-battered London. She was sent to the picturesque town of Bury St Edmunds. She gave birth to Robert William Hoskins on 26 October.

Elsie found the flat expanse of the county of Suffolk, sixty-odd miles outside London, a lonely and depressing place. She was on her own with her newborn baby and, in those days, cockneys were treated with a degree of suspicion and snobbery in rural England. Nanny (our family vernacular for grandmother) decided that she couldn't hang about in the countryside and, after two weeks, they returned to London, Blitz or no Blitz.

Dad's life began in Finsbury Park, in the north London borough of Haringey. At that time the area was solidly working class and fairly deprived. His parents lived in a small one-bedroom flat in Tollington Park. I often pass by the building on the bus. Bob senior and Elsie didn't have much money. Bob was a lorry driver for Pickfords removal company and Elsie a dinner lady at the local school. Dad never had his own bedroom: he slept on the sofa throughout his childhood.

But he always had shoes and a coat and he never went hungry. They were also the only family in the street who had a car, which was practically unheard of for a working-class family at that time.

I've often wondered why living in a flat where their son could have his own room was less of a priority for my grandparents than owning a car. Later in life, when he started to earn serious Hollywood money, Dad had ample opportunity to indulge in the standard trappings of wealth and fame, but he wasn't interested in ostentation. What he craved was space – acres and acres of space. His ultimate aim was to live in a house where every member of the family had the privacy that had been denied him as a child. We eventually moved into a large house on Steeles Road in Belsize Park (coincidentally the street opposite the Load of Hay pub, where my parents first met).

By all accounts, the young Bob Hoskins was a little tyke. Once when he was four, when out shopping in Woolworth's with his mother and her sister, Auntie Nan, he went missing. When she couldn't find him, Elsie wailed, 'My boy! Someone's taken my boy!'

Auntie Nan said, 'If they have they'll soon bring him back.'

Eventually they ended up at the police station.

'Thank the Lord you've come,' said the copper behind the desk. 'He's worse than our Saturday-night drunks.'

An only child, Dad used to spend a lot of time with his cousins Jack and Jean, who were Auntie Nan's kids. Jack matched Dad for naughtiness, and then some.

Jean used to look after Dad, Jack and Valerie, another of their cousins, during the summer holidays. One day she told the boys to watch out for Valerie and stay in the garden so she could go and see her friend. 'When I came back,' she tells me, 'Jack and Bob were gone and they'd tied Valerie to the lamp post.'

Jean remembers how Dad and Jack would stand side by side on the edge of the Caledonian Road to see who could wee the furthest into the traffic.

Less than four months after burying Dad, Mum and I find ourselves at the funeral of Cousin Jack. The funeral is in Loughton and we drive out together; meeting my older half-brother Alex there. Within minutes of arriving at the crematorium, Mum and I greet Jean and her daughters. Jean and Jack were very close.

Dad always maintained that he wouldn't live past the age of seventy-two. He believed that he took after his mother's side of the family, whose mortality was marked by that number. His mother died of cancer at seventy-two; her father died at seventy-two.

I first overheard Dad say this at the age of twelve. It instilled fear in my heart but, on some level, I already knew. I'm sceptical of anyone who claims psychic powers or any form of clairvoyance – it's all a bunch of unsubstantiated piffle as far as I'm concerned – but I did fear my dad's death from an early age.

I've often felt that my family is small. My mum has one sister, Marylyn, who has two children, Natalie and Simon. Because Dad was an only child, I have no first cousins on his side. However, my granddad was one of eight as was Nanny. So there are dozens of cousins and relatives on his side of the family. Dad didn't keep in regular touch with any of them. In fact, he wasn't particularly good at maintaining friendships. If it weren't for my mum making social arrangements, I doubt he'd ever have gone out. Conversely, when he did socialise, he was the life and soul of the party. At his core he was paradoxical, a gregarious loner who was as gentle as he could be overbearing. I think that might be what made his performances so multi-layered and interesting.

The service begins and Jack's friends and family stand up to give their eulogies. They talk of a man who was fun, intelligent, liked a drink and didn't worry what other people thought of him. They could well be talking about Dad.

Looking around this extended family, I recognise Hoskins

family traits: the big, flat ears, the short necks, the broad shoulders, the dark hair, the wide-set eyes.

When your parents are alive, you think you know them. It's only after they die that you realise there is a whole raft of experiences you know nothing about.

When I was growing up, I viewed Granddad and Nanny from a sugar-coated perspective. My little brother Jack and I used to love spending time with them. They were both very creative and made us all sorts of costumes. With them we could be clowns, poodles, superheroes, firemen, doctors or nurses.

Nanny especially is preserved in my memory as a chocolate-box grandmother because she died when I was seven and all my memories are of a sweet, cuddly lady who made me dresses and fed me Bourbon biscuits whenever I went to visit.

The soft, warm-hearted grandmother that I remember had a tough start in life. Her family were poor; her dad was a coalman and he and his wife lived in two rooms in Twyford Street with their eight children. The three boys slept with their parents in one, and their five sisters slept top-to-tail in the other. Jean's mother, Auntie Nan, told her that they were always hungry. 'Granddad was a pig,' she says: 'they'd have bread and dripping and he'd have steak and chips and if he didn't like it he used to chuck it in the fire and sit there and he was the lord.'

Elsie was the youngest and an intelligent child. She passed her eleven-plus to get into grammar school but her parents deliberated about sending her because they couldn't afford the uniform. In the end all her brothers and sisters clubbed together because they wanted her to fulfil her potential. But Elsie didn't want to continue her education, so she went to work instead. She began her working life as a dinner lady in a primary school but gradually worked her way up to become a teacher's assistant.

Elsie married Bob Hoskins senior in 1940 at St Andrew's church, Islington. She was twenty years old and he was twenty-six. Not much is known about Granddad's childhood. There was a rumour that we're descended from Romany Gypsies. Dad used to say he had a Romany collar, by which he meant the hair on his shoulders was in the shape of the wings of a bat. I've no idea if it's true, but I rather like Dad's turn of phrase.

Neither of my grandparents could be described as traditionally good-looking but they cut an alluring dash. They were a glamorous, charismatic couple who loved to go out dancing. Dad often would remember them on one particular occasion, taking to the dance floor at a family wedding. 'I think they fancied themselves to be a cockney version of Fred and Ginger,' he'd say. 'I remember them dancing the tango, and I was mesmerised; they were so graceful. They cleared the floor – everyone else sat down to watch them. When they finished everyone applauded.'

Nanny was a skilled dressmaker. She made lovely gowns to swish around the dance floor and Granddad was always a dapper dresser. Even when he was in his nineties, and came to live with us, he never left the house without his trilby and a perfectly pressed shirt and a tie. He ironed his own clothes and every crease, collar and cuff was perfect.

From the beginning of their marriage, Bob senior always chipped in with his share of the housework (something my dad – a natural cook and fastidious cleaner of the kitchen – inherited from him). He cleaned, washed and ironed clothes and always made sure their flat was spotless. This was very unusual for a man of his generation, but Bob senior was, by all accounts, a rather unusual man.

'He was a funny old sod,' Dad said. 'On the one hand he was a socialist and was very concerned with equality and the rights of working people, but then he'd posh up his accent when he was in what he saw as classy company. He was a devout atheist, and yet superstitious to the core; thirteen people sitting round a table would rattle him like he'd seen a ghost.'

Bob senior was a loving man – exceptionally so for someone from his emotionally repressed generation. When Dad was a little boy, Granddad would sit with him for hours, making him toys out of anything he could find. Once, Granddad made him an entire suit of armour out of an old dustbin. 'It wasn't any old tin-pot thing,' Dad told me. 'It had a proper helmet. I loved it, played in it for hours. You could hear me clanging around Finsbury Park from miles away.'

To my grandparents' eternal credit, they never stifled my dad in any way. Quite the opposite: they encouraged him. They were both very creative and they nurtured the same instinct in their son.

For one family party, to which all the other children going were little girls, Dad got very excited at the prospect of wearing a frilly dress. When his mother produced a sailor suit, he had a fit. 'I was furious,' he said. 'Where was my frock? My mum borrowed one of the neighbours' kids' dresses and I went along to the dance with my girl mates in a frock and a short-back-and-sides haircut. I must have looked like the ugliest child drag queen in the world. I thought I was the business.'

Dad's natural showmanship and confidence came directly from his parents. But they were not without their flaws, like anyone else. Dad described Nanny as being as generous with her beatings as she was with her affection. She could certainly be an overbearing parent, while Granddad was not a strong father figure. When Dad was in his early teens, Granddad handed him the mantle of being the man of the house. Quite literally, Bob senior abdicated responsibility as a father and said to his son, 'You're in charge. You're the dad now.'

Dad dutifully accepted the role of premature adulthood, but he was just a kid and he didn't have a choice. It goes some way to explaining Dad's behaviour later in life. Not only does it account for a lot of his resilience, but to me it also explains the rage that could sometimes bubble over.

He would occasionally become disproportionately angry over a small mishap. For instance, when he made coffee he'd pour too much coffee in the pot, the scalding water would spill on to his hands and he'd smash the whole thing on the kitchen floor in a storm of expletives. After a minute or two he would calm down, mop up the mess and start again.

Once, the kitchen clock fell on his head. It was ten inches in diameter and had an aluminium frame. Mum had taken it down to use in the other room to meditate. She didn't put it back properly, and when Dad went to answer the phone, which was directly under the clock, it fell on his head. There was a skull-shaped dent in the clock from where it landed. I feel sorry for whoever was calling, because Dad went bananas. The caller would have heard some pretty creative swearing. He did see the funny side afterwards, when he'd calmed down and put the clock securely back on the wall.

One of the things I loved about him was that he never held a grudge or indulged in passive-aggressive silence. If he was cross about something he'd get angry and bawl the house down. I can't remember all the specific things that made him angry. It would be over as soon as it began and he'd forget it instantly.

Dad's outbursts could be frightening to those who didn't know him. He was a fiery and passionate personality who sometimes became overexcited. I think people mistook this explosive tendency as violent or threatening. He could certainly turn on his rage for the camera. But for the most part, Dad was gentle, sensitive and bookish, a truth that's at odds with the cockney 'hard man' stereotype.

Despite Dad's subtle, multifaceted and contradictory character, he explained his attitude to things by saying he was 'from the street'. He spent his youth fighting and he was tough. When I asked him why, he replied, 'It's just what you did. You were always fighting, even with your mates. I had plenty of mouth and not a lot to back it up with.'

I find this difficult to understand. Dad provided me with a childhood that was a lot more sheltered and privileged than his; to my middle-class sensibilities, getting into physical fights for no particular reason seems odd. Nonetheless, it was a way of life back then.

Dad's nose was broken in the punch-ups of his youth. During the time I was rummaging around in our family archive, I found a picture of Dad when he was sixteen. He's sitting on a bench next to a girlfriend. He looks very different, as one might expect. But what strikes me most about the image is Dad's nose. It is straight and undamaged, and nothing like the squashed incarnation of it that I knew. I recognise my own nose on his young face, slim at the top descending into a rounded end with a slight ridge at the tip. It's comforting to know that his genes are a part of me for ever, even if it's something as inconsequential as an unbroken nose.

Dad had his demons and looking back on his formative years sheds some light on his later behaviour. His work was his outlet. He often joked that if he hadn't been an actor he would have ended up in prison. I disagree with him on that one – I think Nanny would have hit the roof if he'd ever got into serious trouble. Elsie and Bob senior were respectable working class and drilled firm morals into Dad from an early age. They were a unique, artistic, unconventional family. Dad often said that it was a blessing he was an only child. Nanny and Grand-dad were so proud of him, any other siblings would have had a hard time in his shadow.

CHAPTER THREE

DAD HAD A TENDENCY to embellish the truth and it's sometimes difficult to validate his stories. He was not a liar, but he had a proclivity towards myth-making and when he told a story he believed it to be true.

He first learned the joy of being immersed in a tale at school. Rudyard Kipling's *The Jungle Book* was his favourite; the story of a feral child resonated with him. But he hated school from day one. He went to Stroud Green Secondary Modern and was severely dyslexic – something I have inherited from him. 'Dyslexia wasn't understood at the time,' he said of his schooldays, 'so I was labelled a dunce. Because the teachers thought that I was stupid I was put at the back of the class. What no one knew was that I was short-sighted, so the further away I was from the blackboard, the less chance I had of learning anything.'

I think he found the structure of the classroom stifling. He was too creative and clever to conform to the narrow parameters of a 1950s education. He had an enquiring mind and asked inconvenient questions like 'Is there a God?' and 'What's the meaning of life?' His teachers thought of him as nothing more than a nuisance.

But his schooldays weren't completely wasted, and there was one teacher who encouraged him to fulfil his potential: 'Mr Jones, who taught English, was on my side. He was a big rugby-playing Welshman with a cauliflower ear. He used to say, "Why do you make everybody believe you're such a bad penny, Bob? You're not so bad."'

It was Mr Jones who first turned Dad on to reading. Arthur Conan Doyle, Robert Louis Stevenson, Dickens, Dostoevsky, Tolstoy and Bram Stoker were amongst his favourites.

Dad loved to immerse himself in stories. He enjoyed reading, but he also liked listening to audiobooks. He'd wander around the house in his headphones, plugged into a tale.

When he died, several of the obituaries stated that before falling into acting, Dad tried his hand at many vocations, including fire-eating in the circus, running a nightclub in the East End and working as a window cleaner in a hospital for the criminally insane. I have no idea whether these things are true or not, and it doesn't really matter. It amplifies the Hoskins 'myth' but it doesn't change who he was or what he accomplished.

During my interviews with him when he was ill, we spoke

at length about his time as a porter at Covent Garden fruit and vegetable market, on the high seas with the Norwegian merchant navy and volunteering in a kibbutz. His voice was slow and croaky, but his long-term memory was still reasonably intact and he told me about the years between leaving school and starting out as an actor.

He was fifteen when he left school, with only one O level, in English. His first job was as a porter at Covent Garden market. At that time it was the central supplier of London's flowers and fresh produce. Lorries would roll in from midnight until the small hours of the morning, and the porters were responsible for taking the deliveries of fruit, vegetables and flowers from all over England as well as foreign imports. He worked from midnight every night, heaving boxes from the lorries on to his head. Balancing boxes on flat-capped heads was the standard way to transport heavy loads from one part of the market to another.

It was a vibrant, dynamic place, full of jokes and banter, and Dad had a great time. He said, 'I loved the energy, the characters, the feeling. The smell of the fruit and flowers was intoxicating; really dense. I loved the flavour of the place – everywhere you went you could taste the market – and it was a world that I'd never known before.'

When they took in the deliveries from tropical countries they would sometimes find stowaways in the bananas. One day they found a baby monkey, dead and cold, wrapped around a bunch of bananas as if it were gripping on to its mother. Another time, Dad noticed something out of the corner of his eye. The man he was working with told him to hold still, then plucked a hairy tarantula off his face. They took it to a nearby pet shop and sold it. (He told me that story a few times; it always made me squirm as I'm terrified of spiders.)

Dad's favourite story from his time at Covent Garden was when he witnessed a fight outside the Opera House between a male ballet dancer and a fellow who strolled down the road bellowing homophobic abuse at the man in tights: 'This dancer was standing at the Opera House stage door, calmly looked around at this idiot, stepped towards him, beat seven shades of shit out of him. He then left this guy lying face down on the pavement. I realised then that you should never mess with ballet dancers.'

For as long as I can remember, Dad used to sing little ditties to himself as he bustled around: 'Deedle-i-de-deedle-deedle-i-de-deedle-diddly-i-de-dow-waah . . .' I always assumed it was one of his many idiosyncratic quirks. He would embarrass me terribly when I was a teenager, particularly when I hung out with him on film sets, trying my best to be cool and nonchalant. There Dad would be, in costume, pottering around singing 'Deedle-i-de-deedle-deedle . . .' and cramping my fragile teenage style.

Years later I saw a documentary, filmed in 1957, about the working day of the Covent Garden porters. I was hoping to see a teenage Dad with a stack of boxes on his head but he didn't make an appearance.

However, the men in the film were well versed in 'Deedle-i-de-deedle-deedle-i-de-deedle-diddly-i-de-dow-waah ...' It's an uncanny ghost song. It's comforting to know that Dad's funny melody has an echo in history, accessible on YouTube at the click of a button.

Eventually Dad grew bored of the markets and found himself a job as a galley boy in the Norwegian merchant navy. It was one of the more interesting episodes in his life. He prepared food for the ship and looked after the kitchens, and went all over Europe on the cargo vessel. This gave Dad his first taste of travel.

Once, when the ship was moored in Amsterdam, he became friendly with a dark-haired prostitute called Stella. 'Her pimp kept bashing her up,' he said, 'so I told her she should stop giving him money. One night he got on to the ship with a knife: he was out to cut my throat. Stella had followed him on and punched him square in the face. Knocked him out. They both got chucked off the ship. The next morning we set sail and I never saw her again.'

After a few months at sea, he decided that the sailor's life was not for him and so he returned home to London. Here he tried his hand at several other jobs – steeplejack and window cleaner, to name but two. He also lived in an assortment of flats, drifting from place to place, never putting down roots.

Around this time, Granddad secured a job for Dad at Pickfords, the removals company he worked for, as a trainee accountant. Of all the decisions he made in his life, this is one of the most peculiar. Why anyone thought Dad would make a good accountant is beyond me. Despite his dyslexia, he was actually a strong mathematician, but the monotony of sitting in what was apparently a very tedious office, from nine till five, five days a week, was a recipe for disaster. He was bored out of his skull. Dad had loopy, flamboyant handwriting that he attributed to the three years he spent as a trainee accountant: his ostentatious penmanship was his way of combating the dullness of his day-to-day existence. 'It was the most boring time of my life,' he said, 'and it drove me fucking bananas.'

He walked out of the job right before he was due to qualify as an accountant and hopped on a boat to Israel to volunteer in a kibbutz. (Dad was a restless, impulsive character. Not knowing what was around life's corners made the actor's life perfect for him.) Kibbutz Zikim is only one kilometre from the Gaza Strip in the now-dangerous area of southern Israel. Dad arrived in 1967 and started work picking oranges.

'I buzzed off to Israel,' he told me. 'The kibbutz sounded to me like a good deal – you just turned up there and you worked for them and they looked after you. It was a very primitive set-up, but the countryside was incredible, it was very stark with cultivated fields. I loved it there, learned to drive a tractor. I was good on a tractor. It was one of the biggest adventures of my life.'

I always took this story with a pinch of salt. But after his death, I come across a small brown workbook that even Mum has never seen before. It has Hebrew lettering on the cover and is obviously from an Israeli classroom. Dad's loopy handwriting covers the pages; Hebrew letters with their phonetic sounds next to them in English. The book contains pronouns, key words and phrases: 'Who are you? I am Robert. Where are you from? I am from London. Who is she? She is Hannah. You are Joseph.'

There are passages written in pencil that have faded over the fifty years since they were scrawled down, but there is one page written in pen that can be made out. It is a poem and the earliest example I have found of Dad's writing:

> Come listen to the frantic cries of man
> He's screaming for the thing he doesn't understand.
> He is marching for freedom,
> He is fighting for peace,
> Believing religion to be some kind of release.
> But for him can there be any hope
> When with himself he has never learned?

How long, how long will this grabbing race go on?
How long, how long will they always be so wrong?
How long will it take for him to realise
That his dreams are gained from this shady compromise?

I assume he wrote this as a reaction to the increasing tensions between the Arabs and the Jews. One of the less well-known facts about Dad is that he was a good writer. This poem is a rough precursor to the talent that he honed and polished over the years, but never used to its full potential.

Dad came home from Israel because war was about to break out. Before he left, he spoke to one of the elders at the kibbutz, confiding that he didn't know what to do when he went home to London.

The old man told him, 'It's quite simple. Find something you like doing and then find someone to pay you to do it.'

The story of how Dad fell into acting is possibly the greatest myth of all.

According to legend, not long after his return to London from the kibbutz he accompanied an actor friend to a casting at the Unity Theatre in King's Cross. While his friend was in the casting, Dad propped up the bar and had a few drinks. When someone came out of the room where the auditions were being held and told him that he was up next, he stumbled in and landed the lead.

The hard and fast facts of this story are difficult to verify. Who was his friend? What was the production? What did they ask him to read? These days, the audition process is a tightly reined procedure – actors are cast precisely to type with very little room for manoeuvre. The thought of some bloke wandering in off the street and landing a lead role is astonishing.

The Unity Theatre was formed in the East End of London in 1936 and eventually moved over to Goldington Street, near St Pancras in north London. It originated from the Workers Theatre Movement, which aimed to create plays – often devised by company members – that dealt with the political and social issues of the day, with working-class audiences in mind. If Dad's account of him staggering in and landing a part by accident is indeed true, I can see why he would have landed on his feet. He was as astute and as working class as they came, with a bucketload of charisma and energy.

According to his great friends, the actors Dave Hill and Jane Wood, who Dad first met very shortly after he started acting, he would even adopt other people's stories and make them his own. Dave claims that you could tell him a story and ten minutes later he'd be telling it straight back to you as if it had actually happened to him. 'It could be very disconcerting, but it wasn't game playing. His brain operated in such a way that he would genuinely believe that he had done it himself.' Jane thinks Dad's story about his audition at the Unity Theatre could well be true. It was a left-wing, semi-professional theatre: 'They weren't even paying in those days. It could have happened just the way Bob said it did.'

Another of Dad's long-standing friends is actor Kenneth Cranham. They worked together at the Royal Court, early on in Dad's career. He believes there was something 'fully formed' about Dad as an actor, with everything in place at the time they first met. In no way could he be described as an apprentice. 'It wasn't something he put on, it came from within,' Kenneth says. 'It was natural for him to be on the stage so you never felt any nerves off him.' He thinks Dad was fantastically reliable because as much as he was believable to the audience, he was equally believable to those on stage with him.

One of Dad's defining features was that he didn't give a damn about anyone's opinion. That part of his mind that should have cared about what other people thought was entirely missing. He was fearless and prepared to take risks and it was this, as much as anything, that made a career in acting such a good fit.

Whatever the precise circumstances of Dad's stumble into acting, he was the right person, in the right place, at the right time. I'm glad I'm able to hear and record these stories. It's started to offer me an insight into the eventful forty years before I was born and has made me more curious. I want to find out more.

CHAPTER FOUR

DAD ENTERED THE BUSINESS during an unusual period in history, when actors from working-class backgrounds had an opportunity to break through and make it. The late fifties and early sixties was the era of the kitchen-sink drama: plays and films that hinged on social realism and painted an unflinching picture of working-class British life. Roger Hamer's 1947 film *It Always Rains on Sunday* was the cinematic front-runner, while John Osborne's ground-breaking anti-establishment play *Look Back in Anger* – first staged at the Royal Court in 1956 – made working-class life a subject worthy of examination. In an era where Noël Coward and Terence Rattigan's privileged few lived out their personal dramas in spacious drawing rooms, *Look Back in Anger* was like a cultural earthquake. I've always found this period of history interesting, not only because my dad was a part of it, but because of the seismic shift in the zeitgeist.

Dave Hill and Jane Wood were right there with Dad. There were opportunities for them because they had wonderful writers, writing parts for working-class actors. 'There's no point breaking through barriers if there's nothing to support you,' says Dave. Writers like Shelagh Delaney, Arnold Wesker, Keith Waterhouse, Barry Hines and David Storey gave them a voice.

At that time, every actor worth his salt started out in repertory theatre, touring the country in small-scale productions and learning his craft as he went. It was while Dad was playing in his first job at the Victoria Theatre in Stoke-on-Trent that he met Dave and Jane. They were all appearing in a production of *Romeo and Juliet.* Dave played Prince Escalus, Jane played the Nurse and Dad played Peter, the boy servant, who is usually cut from the play. (Dad used to joke that he hadn't quite learned the rules of the theatre, and during one of the quiet scenes he was backstage and shouted, 'Where's my bleedin' 'at?')

Evenings spent with Dave and Jane make up some of the fondest memories of my early childhood. We must have eaten hundreds of meals around their kitchen table in Belsize Park, all of them laughing and joking about the old days. Theirs and Dad's booming voices would have the place reverberating. In later years, when I went to school, teachers would always tell me to be quiet, but I had grown up with the notion that when people get together, one should speak loud enough to rattle the glass in the windows.

It was during this 1969 production of *Romeo and Juliet* that Dad met the actor, writer and director Ken Campbell. Ken was as anarchic as he was funny and he instantly spotted Dad's talent, despite the fact that he had such a tiny role in the production. He wrote a play for him called *Christopher Pea*. To prepare Dad for the role, Ken sent him around the shops of Hanley in Stoke to learn how to improvise. At a ladies' underwear shop, Ken told him to go in and pretend to be buying a bra for his girlfriend. When the shop assistant asked Dad his girlfriend's bra size, he said, 'Oh, you know, a nice handful.'

When Ken was given a job at the Bolton Octagon Theatre, he asked Dad, Dave and Jane to join him there. They were hired to create what is now known as outreach. They were to take theatre to places in the country where there was none. Together they created several sketches based on urban myths, but the people at the Octagon Theatre thought their ideas were rude, puerile and not very funny, so they all got the sack.

As a result, the Ken Campbell Roadshow came into being. Jane, Dave, Ken and Dad would drive around the country in Ken's beaten-up old camper van. They descended uninvited upon bars, pubs and working-men's clubs to perform sketches in smoky rooms. After each performance a hat would be passed around – it was the acting equivalent of busking. Jane recalls it as the most exciting thing that they could possibly have been doing. They believed if they went in clean to places that weren't theatres – bars and working-men's clubs – they would discover their value as actors, and whether or not acting was something worth doing.

They certainly weren't in it for the money, but whatever

they made had to be enough for them to live off for the rest of the week. Before he met my mum, Dad was terrible with money. He was generous to a fault and would squander his share of the takings. Dave remembers how irresponsible this young version of Dad could be, going to the pub and buying everybody drinks, and then having no money for the rest of the week so that the others would have to keep him. Eventually they settled on a system. Dad would be given an allowance of around £1 a day – at the time enough to eat with, but not much more than that. Dad's generosity was one of his defining qualities. Although he was sometimes reckless in his youth, he'd give you the shirt off his back if he thought you needed it.

Life with the Ken Campbell Roadshow was hand-to-mouth to say the least. If the group ran out of money – which they often did – they would head to Liverpool. Apparently the Liverpudlians were more generous. The group would pitch up and try to do something startling enough to make them turn the jukebox off and pay attention.

Sylvester McCoy, who I've also known all my life, joined the Roadshow later on. He describes to me one of the sketches they regularly performed, called 'The Hitch-hiker'. Dad would play a lorry driver and Dave would be the engine. Dad sat on a seat with Dave on the floor, his back to the audience. Dad would mime getting into the seat, closing the door and then starting the engine. Dave could make great noises like an engine, and Dad did a wonderful mime of a heavy lorry – by the time they'd started up, you could actually see the lorry. Dad would mime turning the wheel and driving along.

Suddenly there would appear a girl hitch-hiking – that was Jane. He'd stop: 'Get in, love. Where you going?' Then Dave would make the engine noises again for laughs, driving along, then he'd stop and declare, 'Sorry, love, I need to go for a wee.' He would get out and then come back in – there would be some comedy around the weeing as well – but Jane would have vanished. He'd mime being a bit worried: they're on a motorway; where did she go?

So being a good man, the lorry driver decides to drive to her house and knocks on the door. That's where Sylvester came in, playing an old man, her father. He'd come out and Dad would say, 'Where is Jane? Did she get back all right?' and Sylvester would say, 'Jane? She's been dead for two years.'

This was acting by the seat of their pants and the perfect outlet for a man as fearless and funny as Dad. One of his tricks, recalled by several people who saw him do it, was to perform an Irish whip, an acrobatic move. He'd shake someone's hand, then do a forward flip and land on his feet, making it look as though the person whose hand he was shaking had thrown him. At other times he would sit in a chair, bounce backwards three times and flip over. Or he'd run up walls, or walk on his hands. When Dave and Jane asked him where he had learned to do that, Dad simply replied, 'In the circus.'

For as long as I can remember, Sylvester McCoy has had problems with his knees and hips. He's had his ankles fused, his hips replaced and now his knees. One day, he realised the reason lay at Dad's feet. Sylvester had never trained or been an actor until he met Dad, and he thought, Ah, what Bob does, that's acting. And so he followed him. 'It was incredibly physical,' he tells me. 'I mean, he was the bravest actor I've ever seen. I thought that's what it was at the beginning, I was so ignorant. I really walked off the street, throwing myself down stairs and hanging out of aeroplanes and escaping from mailbags and straightjackets. All because of Bob Hoskins, because that's what he did.'

They played pubs and working-men's clubs where there were a lot of unhappy people. Because these people were living in misery at the time, the Roadshow went along and tried to make them laugh, Dad especially. 'It was quite astonishing really,' recalls Sylvester, 'to watch him hypnotise the audience and bring them to him in hard, hard areas. I remember we played a working-men's club and they loved us, they just adored us.'

Dad did have a knee replacement in his sixties, but other than that he came out of the Roadshow more or less unscathed.

The Roadshow began to gain in notoriety and William Gaskill, at the time the artistic director of the Royal Court Theatre, came to see for himself what all the fuss was about.

These days, you can't imagine a person who is running a major theatre going to Bolton to see something because they think it might be interesting, but in the early seventies fringe theatre was considered much more significant than it is today.

Gaskill loved what he saw, and the Roadshow was booked to play upstairs at the Royal Court in a festival called 'Come Together', a collection of small shows that had been touring around the country. A bar was built in the studio to replicate the environment the Roadshow actors were used to playing in. They were a huge hit and earned rave reviews; it was the hottest ticket in town, with people fighting tooth and nail to see it.

Along with success at home, the Roadshow started to garner attention abroad, especially in Germany. They spent time in Berlin, and became quite famous in Germany, where they were dubbed 'the Beatles of the Theatre'. Sylvester remembers that Germans would ask them, 'Why do you do this elastic panging?' They would reply that there wasn't any political reason behind it, they were just doing it for a laugh; because Hitler had wiped out variety in the country, as it had featured Jewish people, dwarves and homosexuals, and that had been considered decadent in Nazi eyes. The Roadshow arriving in Germany represented a new generation that hadn't been seen and they blew audiences away. They were successful, but at the same time the audience couldn't quite work out why they did what they did, except to have a laugh. It left audiences puzzled.

They would perform the shows, people would love them and take them out for meals. 'It was great fun,' says Sylvester, 'because the wall was up, Checkpoint Charlie was there, spies were still around and the whole place had that wonderful John le Carré atmosphere.' They were taken down into dark cafes: 'People had plans, revolutions, smoke everywhere.' They found it very exciting, but they were also quite tired. 'Bob was so tired he fell asleep on a plate of tripe. Suddenly he woke up and said, "My balls!"'

The success of the Ken Campbell Roadshow led to major parts for Dad: a studio production of Bertolt Brecht's *The Baby Elephant* and then, on the Royal Court's main stage, in premieres of Edward Bond's *Lear* (1971), with Harry Andrews, and Charles Wood's *Veterans* (1972), opposite Sir John Gielgud.

Dad had some great stories about his time working with John Gielgud. One night, he invited Dad out for dinner. 'My dear boy, you're looking terribly thin,' he said. 'You must let me buy you a decent meal.' At this point in his life my dad lived in a beaten-up leather jacket and scruffy jeans. He asked one of the other actors if he could borrow a suit as Gielgud had invited him out to a fancy restaurant. Unfortunately, the actor was tall and thin and the suit was a terrible fit. Dad arrived at John Gielgud's house, bursting out of the suit that was cut for someone with the body of a pipe cleaner. Gielgud took one look at him and said, 'Do put the leather jacket back on, dear heart. It's far better for my image.'

Dad learned a lot from working with such a skilled actor. At one point, Gielgud took him aside to give him advice on how to get a laugh. 'He told me to step back, count to two, and then deliver the line,' Dad said. 'Well, I did it, and I got a round [of applause] every night. I tried to do it again on another job and got fuck all!'

Round or no round, Dad's star had begun to rise. Funny, popular and anarchic with a raw gift, he was admired and liked by everyone. He was also rather crazy and wild, which served him well as an actor. According to Dave, 'He was quite mad, but mad in that glorious way that meant he could totally believe in whatever he was doing.'

To truly succeed, an actor – regardless of how much talent he has – needs to have gritty determination. Dad could hustle as well as, if not better than, anyone. According to Barry Hanson, producer of *The Long Good Friday*, he simply never took no for an answer.

When they first met at the Royal Court, Barry was director of the Hull Arts Centre. Dad called him on the phone and told him he would be joining Barry at the theatre. 'I'm gonna turn up on Monday,' he said.

Barry told him, 'Bob, I'm not doing anything on Monday.'

But Dad turned up anyway.

They were doing Harold Pinter's *The Homecoming.* Barry says, 'He basically told me that he was going to play Lenny and, I must say, he was brilliant; very, very frightening and very, very funny.'

Barry also cast Dad as Richard III and King Lear. It's hard to imagine in today's world that a relatively inexperienced and untrained actor could barge into a theatre and win meaty, leading parts, but it was certainly phenomenal training. It's a crying shame that the repertory system fell apart in the eighties.

In many ways, Dad's cinema career overshadowed his successes on stage. Many people don't even know what a prolific stage actor he was, but some of his best work was done in the theatre.

He worked with Kenneth Cranham in a play called *Geography of a Horse Dreamer,* written and directed by Sam Shepard. It was performed in the Jerwood Theatre Upstairs at the Royal Court. It was the first thing Sam Shepard had ever directed, so it was new territory for him. Kenneth recalls that Shepard was terribly pleased with them and with how quickly they worked. (Apparently this stemmed from the fact that American actors often won't learn their lines until they're in make-up, while British actors come from an old tradition of being grateful and will learn all the lines quickly.)

Kenneth and Dad were sharing a dressing room and Kenneth had decided he wanted to play his character with Dick

Tracy eyebrows. He put Sellotape on his head to create the shape of the eyebrow and filled in with black in between. 'I used to love doing the make-up,' he says, 'and I'd give myself the best jawline in existence. Just the whole business of it, it's quite therapeutic.' But Dad didn't do anything. One night he looked over at Kenneth, doing his eyebrows, and told him, 'It ain't fucking *Dracula*, you know!'

Later, in 1974, Dad played Alfred Doolittle in George Bernard Shaw's *Pygmalion* with Diana Rigg at the Albery Theatre. A major Royal Shakespeare Company season at the Aldwych followed in 1976. One reviewer commented on his 'earthy muscle' in Eugene O'Neill's *The Iceman Cometh* and Shaw's *The Devil's Disciple*. A few months before he met my mum in the Load of Hay pub, she saw him perform in a production of John Webster's *The Duchess of Malfi* with Helen Mirren at the Roundhouse in Camden.

I wish I'd seen him as Nathan Detroit in Richard Eyre's staging of *Guys and Dolls* at the National Theatre in 1982. I've met many people in the business who credit the show and Dad's performance as their inspiration for wanting to either act, write or direct. My maternal grandfather often talked about how he had cried in public only twice: when England won the World Cup in 1966, and during *Guys and Dolls* when he saw 'Sit Down, You're Rockin' the Boat'.

I only saw Dad perform on stage twice: in *Old Wicked Songs* by Jon Marans in 1996, and then in 2005 in Luigi Pirandello's *As You Desire Me.* I enjoyed watching him in both productions, but I missed out on the golden performances of his youth. However, there was one incident during *Old Wicked Songs* which always makes me laugh whenever I think of it. One night, stage management forgot to set the pills on stage for the scene when Dad's character, Mashkan, attempts suicide. Dad improvised by trying to strangle himself with his bare hands. The curtain went down to him convulsing on the floor.

As a family we would go to the theatre regularly. Then we'd go for dinner and discuss the production. It became a family ritual that I loved and dearly miss.

According to Dad, he only got into film and television because he thought it would help give him a leg-up in the theatre. He'd noticed that anybody who had made a TV programme or a film always got the best parts, regardless of talent. He went for telly jobs thinking it would help his theatre work, but once he found himself in front of a camera, he realised this was the way forward for him.

In the early seventies Dad decided he wanted Sally Hope to be his new agent. True to form, he marched into her office with his head shot and announced that she would be signing him. Dad started to get small television roles, gradually working his way up to bigger parts in *Thick as Thieves* with John Thaw and playing the lead role, Alf, with Donald Gee, in *On the Move*, an educational programme for adult literacy that became a much-loved show.

But it was a musical drama called *Pennies from Heaven*, a six-part BBC series written by Dennis Potter, that proved to be his big break in 1978. He was thirty-five years old. Set in 1930s England, *Pennies from Heaven* tells the story of Arthur Parker, a sheet-music salesman who travels around the country trying, unsuccessfully, to sell his wares. Arthur is married to repressed Joan (played by Gemma Craven), but he is a passionate man and finds their life dreary and unfulfilling. To escape the boredom, Arthur often loses himself in romantic reverie, with mimed musical sequences playing out the yearnings of his imagination. For the first musical number in the opening episode, Arthur, whose morning advances have been rebuffed by his wife, gets out of bed and turns to the window, where a golden light streams through. He mimes to Elsie Carlisle's 'The Clouds Will Soon Roll By'. For a masculine man like my dad to burst into a woman's song signalled the beginning of a whole new future.

There was a heightened reality to the series, and Dad's background in the theatre served him well. However, he hadn't been first choice for Arthur. On a visit to his lovely Victorian house in south London, *Pennies from Heaven* director Piers Haggard explains to me that they had narrowed the casting down to Michael Elphick. But then the producer, Kenith Trodd, said, 'I just want you to see somebody else . . .' So they met Dad and decided he was just right for the part. 'It seemed to fit him,' says Piers: 'he could be it, he didn't really have to act it. Arthur is sexy, cheeky, a great con man, a real mixture. Bob was perfect.'

It's often been said that Dad never seemed to be acting, that he just inhabited the parts as himself rather than trying to impose an unnatural artifice on to his own character. He had the ability to make a part his own, to incorporate the character's story into his own personal narrative. And yet he was no Method actor. In fact, he found most traditional acting techniques pretentious and unnecessary. He used to say that actors who occupied themselves with various methodologies wanted to 'look busy' or 'impress the boss'. When I was studying acting at university, we would discuss various acting approaches. I remember him talking about Stanislavsky's system. He had once read about it and thought it was 'just obvious, really'. Then he'd read about Lee Strasberg and the Method and thought it 'a load of old bollocks'.

I loved those conversations Dad and I had about acting. His approach was simple, sensitive and intelligent. He used to say that drama is about the quiet, private moments you deal with alone. He also explained how women were a huge influence on him. 'I realised one day,' he said, 'that men are emotional cripples. We can't express ourselves emotionally; we can only do it with anger and humour. Emotional stability and expression comes from women.'

Dad grew up surrounded by strong women. Nanny and her sisters adored him, but they wouldn't have stood for any nonsense. It was from women that he learned about acting. He used to study them, study their reactions. 'I started my career by becoming a stalker,' he said, 'watching women in the street, the way they greet each other. I thought if I could capture some of that expression, that depth of emotion, it will make me interesting as an actor.'

I think this goes some way to explaining Dad's breadth and sensitivity. His portrayal of Arthur is heartbreaking. A simple man driven by instinct and sexuality, he longs for spiritual fulfilment. He's groping for something like religion.

Acting was the easy part in *Pennies from Heaven*: it was the dancing and musical numbers that proved a bit more challenging. Despite his natural affinity for acrobatics, Dad's short legs and stumpy fingers weren't built for dance. He worked incredibly hard to master the dancing – hours and hours a day working with the choreographer Tudor Davies. 'I thought I was like Fred Astaire,' he later told my mum. 'But when I saw the rushes I realised that I looked like a baby hippo.'

• • •

Pennies from Heaven was a big success and Dad's career really began to take off. Roles in films were just around the corner. One day around that time, he was driving down Tottenham Court Road when he saw a familiar figure in a trilby hat standing underneath a huge poster of Dad, telling passers-by, 'That's my son.' Dad screeched to a stop and bundled Granddad into the car.

People have often asked me if I find it strange watching Dad on screen. The answer is an obvious no, because it's all I've ever known. However, I rarely watched his performances more than once, mostly because Dad was totally disinterested in watching himself. So it would come as something of a surprise to people when I told them I had never watched *Pennies from Heaven*. I bought the box set from HMV when I was about twenty-one and had every intention of watching it, but I never quite got around to it. In fact, when I got home I suggested that we all sit down and watch it together, as a family, but Dad was much less enthusiastic. The box set ended up at the back of a cupboard, entirely forgotten.

CHAPTER FIVE

MY DAD USED TO describe himself as 'five foot six cubic' and not your typical movie star. Because he had no hang-ups about the way he looked, he would be the first to poke fun at himself. Credit for this should go largely to Nanny and Granddad. Nanny especially imbued Dad with the confidence never to care what other people thought of him. 'If anyone doesn't like you,' she would tell him, 'they're either stupid, blind or they've got bad taste.' It was a mantra he repeated to me throughout my life.

And Dad was no fool. He knew that, in lots of ways, his looks were his secret weapon. In the theatre, certainly, his shape worked to his complete advantage. 'People remembered me,' he said. 'You'd get these very tall, sort of graceful people with wonderful voices and then I'd walk on, this cube, and everyone would say, "Who's that?"'

'The moment I met him I knew that here was a film actor,' remembers John Mackenzie, director of *The Long Good Friday*. For both of them this was to be their breakout film, and it marked the beginning of a lifelong friendship. John and Dad shared an anarchic sense of humour and a hunger for know-ledge. Both were devoted to their families and enjoyed a drink. The house would fill with laughter whenever John and his wife Wendy came for dinner.

The Long Good Friday was scripted by Barrie Keeffe. When the film was conceived in 1979 the Thatcher era was only a few months old, and yet the story is eerie in its prescience about the political, historical and social landscape looming in the near future.

Having worked with Dad in the theatre, producer Barry Hanson had experienced his talent first-hand. From the beginning he was first choice for the role of Harold Shand, a darkly funny gangster with a thriving criminal empire. Barrie Keeffe also had Dad in mind for the lead. When they first met with Dad for a script discussion, he was just back from South Africa, where he had been filming *Zulu Dawn*. The meeting took place at the London School of Hygiene and Tropical Medicine, because he'd managed to get ill with a massive tapeworm during filming. When they were allowed into Dad's room, the doctors warned Keeffe, Hanson and Mackenzie in no uncertain terms that they mustn't get him too excited about the script because they would be operating on him the next day, and if he got too excited the tapeworm might split in two. Dad got excited; fortunately the tapeworm didn't.

The Long Good Friday spans one disastrous day in Shand's

life. His plan is to redevelop the Docklands of east London for a future Olympic Games, and in order to do so he decides to go into business with representatives from the New York Mafia. Gradually his world is torn apart by a series of murders and bombs, perpetrated by an unseen foe. Shand and his henchmen try to uncover his attacker's identity. Eventually he approaches the local IRA members he suspects of orchestrating the violence against him, and kills them. After the murders, the Mafia representatives decide against working with Shand.

The last shot of the film is of Shand in the back of his car, which has been hijacked by IRA terrorists. Shand is silent, yet his face displays a huge range of emotions; immediate shock gives way to horror, fury, self-reflection and then finally sad acceptance.

Dad often used to speak about how that scene taught him everything he ever needed to know about film acting. 'For that last shot, John Mackenzie said, "I'm going to put the camera on your face, Bob, for five minutes and I don't want you to say a word; I just want you to think your way through the film." I said to him, "That's a joke, you'll kill the film," and John said, "What you've got to learn, Bob, is that the camera can read your mind. It can see what you think."'

Dad could take any character, develop a deep insight into their personality and also sympathise with their predicament. Harold Shand has a deep well of vulnerability beneath his bullish exterior. He's a savage, murderous criminal, yet whenever I watch the film I find myself rooting for him. Dad said, 'I was presented with a character that acts tough but is doubtful inside. John taught me that there can be several levels to a character. He also taught me that, if you are thinking the character's thoughts, whatever you are doing is right. And that basically made my film career.'

There are a number of lines of dialogue in *The Long Good Friday* that are pure Dad. When Shand's best friend has been stabbed in a swimming pool, his body is stored in an ice-cream van to avoid suspicion. 'There's a lot of dignity in that, isn't there?' he says. 'Going out like a raspberry ripple.' Or when Shand is trying to find out information about who's persecuting him: 'No one's heard anything?' he asks. 'That just ain't natural. It's like one of them silent, deadly farts. No clue then – *pow!* – you go cross-eyed.'

I have no idea if these lines were in the original script. I often wonder if they were added by the sarcastic, irreverent man I knew. That surreal turn of phrase and gallows humour is him down to a T.

Sally Hope, Dad's agent at the time, recalls the collaborative nature of the project. Every Sunday for several months prior to shooting, Dad, John Mackenzie, Barry Hanson and Barrie Keeffe would meet at her house to work on the script. 'Every time a new part of the script was written, Bob would read it,' Sally remembers. 'It was then that you realised how he could make the part sing.'

John Mackenzie agrees that Dad created that role. 'Absolutely,' he says. 'He burns the celluloid, as they say.'

According to his fellow actor Ray Winstone – a long-time friend who first met Dad on a short film called *My Father the Liar* on which Dad was the director (part of the 1999 collection *Tube Tales*) – *The Long Good Friday* is as important a film as Martin Scorsese's *Raging Bull*. '*Raging Bull* is not a movie about boxing,' Ray says. 'It's about a person who just happens to be a boxer. And *The Long Good Friday* is a film about a person who just happens to be a gangster. For that reason, more than any other, it is without a shadow of a doubt the best British gangster film ever made. And that,' he adds, 'is solely down to Bob's performance.'

Ray believes it to be the most modern performance you'll ever see. 'People are trying to do that now,' he says, 'trying to work at making everything natural, and yet he was doing that – without even trying – in 1979. That's why the film doesn't date, you see? That performance will stand up for the rest of time.'

The story of *The Long Good Friday* didn't end when the film wrapped. Lew Grade at ITV had financed it – to the tune of almost a million pounds – for screening on television. When he watched the film he was horrified by the violence and politics and refused to screen it on television unless it could be changed extensively. He also refused to release it in the cinema. It looked as if the film would never see the light of day. Fortunately, however, it was eventually bought from Lew Grade by George Harrison's company, HandMade Films.

The film had great success at the box office and there was interest in releasing it in America. It was decided that Dad's voice should be dubbed: the general consensus was that his cockney accent would be difficult for an American audience to understand. But no one thought to mention this to Dad, who was furious. 'It was in my contract that they couldn't dub me without my permission, and they did,' he explained. 'They actually said to me, "Listen, Bob, we think you'll like it – we ain't half done it well." So me and Sally went to see the film, and it was dubbed in a Wolverhampton accent. I saw ten minutes of it and got up and said, "You're fucking nicked." The frightening thing was that it was brilliantly, brilliantly dubbed. But it had no comedy in it any more – no life.'

Dad applied for an injunction to prevent the dubbed version from being used. The injunction was upheld and the film was released in its original form, which in turn brought Dad to the attention of Hollywood.

However much success came his way, Dad never abandoned his working-class roots. He had a strong sense of his own identity – who he was and where he came from – and he never attempted to be anyone other than himself.

Dad was never especially interested in awards and accolades. I'm sure whenever he did win something it'd be very exciting and he'd have been pleased. But as a general rule he didn't require external validation because he already knew his worth. He probably could have chosen more projects that may have been more likely to earn awards, but he didn't waste energy on regrets. He was nominated for a BAFTA for *The Long Good Friday* – I'm sure he wasn't bothered about not winning.

After his death, there is an expectation that the business will pay tribute to him at award ceremonies. There is quite a fuss in February 2015 when BAFTA omits him from the memorial reel shown during the annual British Academy Film Awards. He is mentioned in the 2014 BAFTA Television Awards, held on 18 May. After the complaints made by members of the public and Dad's old colleagues, BAFTA release a statement explaining that they had mentioned him at the TV ceremony, as it was shortly after his death. They go on to say they only pay tribute to people once. However, all this would have meant nothing to him.

I imagine him sitting with me at my kitchen table now, where we sat together so many times, drinking endless cups of tea. If I were to say, 'Hey, Dad, BAFTA snubbed you,' he would look up from his paper, shrug his shoulders, quietly say 'Fuck 'em' and go back to reading the news.

This isn't to say that he was never pleased to win awards. His last award was an Emmy in 2010, for his performance in Jimmy McGovern's BBC drama *The Street*. He was happy about winning, but in the same way you'd be happy if you were to receive an unexpected tax rebate. I don't remember him discussing it in any great detail. Perhaps his attitude was different when he was younger, with more to prove, more to gain. However, he still would have taken it all with a big pinch of salt. He loved the business and his work, but he kept it in perspective and recognised it for the 'cobblers' that it is.

A few weeks ago Mum took all his awards out of the cupboard where they've been stored for a few years. She laid them out on the floor of her living room and Ray Ward, who's worked for my parents for many years, polished them, restoring their former shine. When they were spread out they nearly covered the entire carpet. I hadn't realised there were so many. Mum then carefully packed them all up in bubble wrap and put them away again.

When an actor is nominated for an award, they're usually obliged to show up at the ceremony. Dad found red-carpet events tedious, although he would go along to them to fulfil his professional commitments. But, given the choice, he'd prefer to stay home and cook a nice meal with Mum and watch a documentary about ancient Greek civilisation.

And he always made it clear to the powers that be that he would never accept any honours. He was often asked in interviews about the possibility of a knighthood – many of his contemporaries were knights and dames, and journalists would assume that he would like the same privilege.

When one asked about it, Dad said, 'Not a chance. I wouldn't know who I was. I'd wake up as Sir Bob and have no idea who Sir Bob was.'

The journalist then asked if my mum would like to be a lady. Dad replied, 'She already is.'

He wasn't aggressive in his dismissal of honours from the queen. He didn't think any less of those who accepted knighthoods – it just wasn't for him.

After he announced his retirement in 2012, he received a letter offering him a CBE but he declined.

It was 29 July 1981, a Wednesday, and it was a national holiday. On that day, in the blazing summer sunshine, Prince Charles married Lady Diana Spencer. The royal wedding was a huge event in London: there was a festive atmosphere in the city and all the pubs stayed open late. My mum was out with her teacher colleagues in the Load of Hay pub on Haverstock Hill, just up the road from Haverstock Comprehensive School, where she taught sociology.

Born in Bristol into a working-class family, Mum left school at sixteen and went to work, like most people of her background and generation. She was and still is a very intelligent woman, and at the age of twenty-two, bored by her job, she moved to London and went on to pursue higher education at Goldsmith's College. After she graduated with a BA in sociology, she became a secondary schoolteacher.

She was standing at the bar with a group of friends when outside a troop of morris dancers jangled their way past the pub. Her friends hurried out to watch the stick-waving dancers, but Mum wasn't interested and remained at the bar. She looked across the smoky room and saw a face she recognised. The actor Bob Hoskins was sitting on a bench opposite.

He smiled at her, and she smiled back. He was with Ken Campbell – they strolled over and struck up a conversation. Mum played it very cool and showed no sign of being starstruck, even though she knew exactly who he was. When asked what she did for work, Mum replied that she was a schoolteacher. Ken launched into a tirade about the flawed ethos of the education system. With composure and self-assurance, Mum pointed out all the ways in which he was mistaken. My dad was smitten.

In later years, Dad spoke of this first meeting with her as though he'd strutted over, laid on the old cockney charm and sauntered off in a blaze of glory. But Mum told me her first impression of him was that he was very vulnerable. Underneath his bravado, he was shy and sensitive and Mum spotted it straight away. The connection between them was instant and profound.

Generally, Dad didn't give two hoots about what anyone thought of him, but Mum's opinion was important. When they met, *The Long Good Friday* had been in cinemas for a year, but Mum hadn't seen it. Dad found a cinema where it was still playing – the Phoenix in East Finchley – and drove her there in his jeep. She went in to watch the film on her own and he waited anxiously for her to come out.

To outside eyes, it might have appeared that Mum had hit the marital jackpot. Dad was a famous actor about to make it big. After they got together, some of Mum's friends became distant. She found herself left off the guest lists of a few weddings and parties, and one friend dropped out of her life altogether. She was hurt by these rejections. After all, she hadn't changed – it was just her circumstances. Dad pointed out that as far as her friends were concerned, she might as well have moved to Mars.

When I interview Dad's old friends and colleagues, they all voice similar opinions about Dad as an actor and as a man. Everyone I speak to who knew Dad before he met Mum says how glad they were when Mum and Dad got together. Sylvester McCoy, his old friend from the days of the Ken Campbell

Roadshow, goes as far as to say she saved him. I find this very touching, and I can well believe it. Dave Hill tells me that Dad got himself a sensible woman, and that she sorted him out.

It would seem Dad's friends breathed a collective sigh of relief. John Mackenzie in particular was delighted that they got together. John and Dad were very close, and I think John sometimes worried about Dad's self-destructive streak. Mum had no intention of saving Dad and she didn't see him as someone who needed fixing. But from the outside, everyone could see how happy and settled Dad became after they met.

My parents married in 1982, the same year Dad was in Richard Eyre's National Theatre hit production of *Guys and Dolls* as Nathan Detroit, opposite Julia McKenzie as Miss Adelaide. Mum always said it was a brilliant show.

The cast and crew threw Mum and Dad a party a week before their wedding. Richard Eyre phoned Mum and asked them to meet him in the bar for a drink in the green room on the Saturday evening. They were sitting in the bar, chatting, when Kevin Williams, who played the rude waiter in the show, appeared in costume and in character and served them champagne on a tray. Mum thought it was a bit unusual, but no one else took any notice.

Then a piper in full Highland dress walked into the bar

and began to play. Richard Eyre ushered Mum and Dad to follow the piper into one of the large rehearsal rooms near the green room. When they entered, they were met with a wave of tumultuous applause from the cast and crew of the show.

The entire room was laid out like a cabaret: there was a stage at one end, and above it was draped a huge piece of sheet declaring 'Congratulations Linda and Bob!' Mum and Dad were bowled over by the huge amount of effort everybody had obviously put in. In the middle of the floor was a table laid out for a dinner, complete with Julia McKenzie's candelabra. The whole cast performed pieces they'd composed themselves.

The music and dancing went on long into the night. Mum still remembers the pile of wedding presents. 'The boxes were all wrapped up in white paper, black paper, to make them look like dice to coincide with Dad's part in the show,' she says. 'It was a wonderful evening.'

By all accounts, my parents' wedding was a riotous, joyful affair. Neither of them was particularly religious so they didn't wish to get married in a church. But then Dad and Dave Hill went to look at Finsbury Town Hall with a view to booking a ceremony, but found it to be a hideous, miserable place, so Dad went back to the drawing board. Eventually he went into Islington Central Methodist Church, a funny little oblong of a building that Dad likened to a Mars bar. The pastor there was more than happy to conduct the service. Dad came clean about his lack of faith but the pastor didn't seem to mind in the slightest.

The day arrived. Dad wore the same white suit he wears in the opening scene of *The Long Good Friday*. Mum wore a chic dropped-waist 1920s-inspired lace dress. 'It wasn't at all posh,' Mum says. 'In the morning we were all cutting up vegetables for the salads, which we served in washing-up bowls.' They had no money, so the wedding was a collective effort: the National Theatre props department made a huge spit on which a massive side of beef was cooked in the garden, and Dave Hill took charge from the early morning onwards.

Actor Gawn Grainger was Dad's best man. Dad went over to Gawn's house the night before the wedding, and they tried to avoid the press, who were on to it. They spent a very quiet, pleasant evening with a few drinks in the house, nothing wild.

In the morning, before they went out, Gawn asked, 'Well, shall we go for a drink?'

Dad said, 'No, I want to do one thing in particular.'

'What's that?' said Gawn.

'I want to go to Marine Ices and have ice cream.'

So off they went.

I find this really funny and typical of Dad's mercurial nature. When Jack and I were children, Mum and Dad took us to Marine Ices in Chalk Farm on Saturday nights.

Gawn tells me Dad wanted ice cream instead of a pre-wedding drink because he wanted to be in control of the day. 'It was extraordinary,' he says, 'but he wasn't going to get out of his nut.'

Dad and Mum had the ceremony in the Mars bar church, and when they walked back down the aisle after tying the knot everybody stood up and clapped. Afterwards everyone trooped back to their house in Penn Road. Mum and Dad had plans at the time to gut the house and do it all up, so it was a rather shabby blank canvas. They'd bought marker pens and all the guests graffitied the house. By all accounts it was a great party. Music was provided by the National Theatre – John Tams was musical director at the time – and they performed folk wedding songs. At one point some kids got hold of a bucket of water, with a long rope, and dangled it from an upstairs window over the guests in the garden. 'It was anarchic,' Mum remembers, 'but so much fun.'

When I leaf through my parents' wedding album, I think they look completely happy: laughing and dancing with unreserved joy. I also pick up a sense of relief in their faces. It's as though they're saying to each other: 'Ah, there you are! Thank God you turned up – I thought I'd never meet you.'

From the outset it was clear to everyone who knew them that Mum was the right match for Dad. Where he was garrulous, she was refined. Where he was extravagant, she was restrained. They shared a sense of humour and, even though their paths in life had been very different, they both hailed from solid, working-class backgrounds, and had then gone on to do something unusual. They understood each other; they could spend hours together in an easy, companionable silence.

In the space of less than two years, their lives had changed immeasurably. Within that time they met, were married, I was born and we had all moved across the world.

CHAPTER SIX

I WAS BORN ON 27 May 1983, just less than a year after my parents' wedding. Dad always said I came out talking. I was the spitting image of him. I have pictures of him holding me when I'm a week old and I look like a little bruiser. We have a matching receding hairline, set jaw and clenched fists – I look like someone has carved a Bob Hoskins doll out of pink rubber. There are a few shots of me in a frilly baby hat, but it does nothing to soften the unmistakable Hoskins looks.

Two months after I showed up, Dad was offered a part in *The Cotton Club*, Francis Ford Coppola's film about the famous New York jazz club. In it he played Owney Madden, the mobster owner of the Cotton Club, where Dixie Dwyer, played by Richard Gere, is a handsome young cornet player. Dad got a call about the film on a Friday and was in New York on the Monday. Shortly afterwards, Mum flew over with me. She had gone from being a single sociology teacher in London to marrying the love of her life, having a baby and moving to New York.

Dad was working long hours – he'd be gone first thing in the morning and wouldn't get back until late in the evenings.

Mum didn't know a soul and would push me around the city's streets in a pram, but she was never lonely. She found that passers-by were jovial and friendly and would strike up conversations. 'Oh, what a beautiful baby boy!' was usually their opening line. When Mum replied that I was actually a girl, her English accent would encourage even more interest.

Mum and Dad always spoke very fondly of their time in New York. It was a period of great excitement and they enjoyed living in Greenwich Village. As they had a similar sense of humour, there was comedy value to be found in being Brits abroad. Once, when she was out shopping for Dad's supper, as she did every day – usually in a great Italian deli off Sixth Avenue – Mum went into a hardware store and asked for a spanner. The man behind the counter was mystified by her request. He was so flummoxed, in fact, that she had to draw him a picture. 'Oh!' he cried. 'You mean a wrench!' This went on everywhere. Their favourite was the time Dad went into a liquor store and asked for a 'pack of fags'.

When Mum and Dad would go out for dinner, they'd take me with them. John Mackenzie was in town at the time, and would often come too. One outing to a Vietnamese restaurant was almost ruined by my fractious, grizzly state. But then a waitress scooped me up and took me outside. Mum was horrified, thinking the girl had run off with me. But she was very grateful a few moments later when the waitress returned with a much calmer, sleepier baby.

The Cotton Club wasn't a great commercial success, but Dad's performance was well reviewed and I think it helped to open a few doors for him.

Over the next few years, we travelled everywhere with Dad. Shortly after we returned from New York, we all went to Italy, where he was playing the title role in *Mussolini and I*, which also starred Anthony Hopkins and Susan Sarandon. We travelled throughout Italy, basically following the locations where Mussolini had lived.

Starting at Lake Garda, we then went on to Verona, Merano and Fregene. We were in a large hotel by Lake Garda one Sunday morning when I slipped in the bathroom and Dad, in trying to help me, accidentally pulled my arm out of its socket. Mum tells me that it was hanging at a horrible angle, so they took me to the hospital. The crew found out what had happened and about twenty of them showed up in Accident and Emergency. They were very attentive, all alarmed by the state of my arm, but a doctor popped it back in quick enough.

A week or so later was my first birthday. Dad told the crew that we would be having dinner in the hotel that evening and a load of them turned up to celebrate. 'You sat at the head of the table,' Mum says, 'holding court and eating spaghetti. You only had two teeth at the bottom front and pasta would hang on either side.' Then a beautiful cake arrived with one candle, at which point the entire crew broke into an operatic, sonorous rendition of 'Happy Birthday' in Italian.

My very earliest memory is of having my first ice cream in Italy. Dad told me how a bunch of them were having gelato and that I looked very miffed at being excluded. He bought me one, and I can remember being handed a cone filled with fruits of the forest ice cream that seemed bigger than my head.

During this trip, we spent some time in Rome. Mum and Dad met up with Richard Gere, who they knew not only from *The Cotton Club* but also from the film *The Honorary Consul* (also released as *Beyond the Limit*), directed by John Mackenzie. They'd all spent time together in Mexico when filming; Mum had been pregnant with me at the time.

Richard Gere had tickets one evening to a Bob Dylan concert and invited them along. My parents left me with a babysitter and they all went off in a car. The concert was at a football stadium. When they arrived, they were given seats on the edge of the stage, sitting beside Carlos Santana, and they watched Dylan sing. 'It was extraordinary,' Mum says. 'The audience were holding up their lighters. The energy that came off Dylan almost knocked us off the stage.'

• • •

When Mum and Dad first met, he told her that he didn't want to get remarried or have any more children. However, within a few weeks he'd changed his tune. I suppose once he met the right woman he realised family life was actually something he craved. Mum was very clear about what she wanted. She was in her mid-thirties when they met: she told him she wanted two babies before she was forty. So Jack arrived hot on my heels, born only twenty-two months after me.

When Mum was pregnant with Jack, she took me to Australia to visit Dad in Melbourne. He was filming *The Dunera Boys*, a TV series about Jewish emigrants who were shipped to Australia in the 1940s. According to Mum, we had a great time in Melbourne, although I was at an age where they couldn't afford to take their eyes off me for a minute.

Dad often told a story about when they took me to a petting zoo and I tried to climb on to a wallaby. (I was rather precocious and interested in everything and everyone.) I have a few brilliant photos of Dad and me in a park. Dad has me in a little toddler harness and I'm leading him up a very steep boulder. He has a hanky tied in four knots on his head, looking every inch the typical Brit abroad. I'm wearing a pair of red dungarees and a white T-shirt. We look a very odd little pair.

Although they enjoyed themselves in Australia, Mum found it quite challenging, dealing with being pregnant as well as having a toddler who would never settle. Apparently I couldn't get used to the time difference and never would sleep through the night.

On the flight home I was fractious and disturbed a woman sitting in front of us. She turned around in her seat and screeched at Mum: 'I haven't paid good money to sit in business class only to be disturbed by your little brat!'

Mum was so overtired that she burst into tears.

A woman behind her reached out and put a hand on Mum's shoulder in solidarity. The cabin crew rushed over to Mum with a box of tissues and a glass of water. There were a lot of Aussie businessmen in the cabin. One of them called over: 'Don't worry about her. She'll never know what it's like to have kids because she's too fat and ugly to ever get married!'

Before Jack and I started school, we went everywhere with Dad. I became accustomed to planes and jet lag from an early age. However, there were still periods when we'd be apart from him. Mum tells me that she could feel the pain radiating off me, even when I was a tiny baby. 'You were so connected with him, when he was gone you missed him terribly.'

On 5 March 1985 Jack was born. The closeness in our age made it possible for us to live the life we did. We often travelled with Dad and because there was less than two years between us, my parents could take us to the same activities, restaurants and films.

When Jack was a baby, Dad and I spent a lot of time together. He'd bundle me up in his car and take me on day trips. When I rummage through our vast collection of family photos, I find hundreds of shots of me as a toddler, in assorted eccentric outfits, at the park, at the zoo, and putting the final touches to a rather stocky snowman. As I pore over the images, I gain a deeper insight into our bond. He was not a perfect parent (who is?), but he gave me so much of his time and attention.

Once, when I was about two-and-a-half, Dad planted pumpkins in the vegetable patch in the garden. We tended the vegetables until they were huge, bulbous and a vivid shade of orange. He decided it was time to harvest them and we would bake a pie.

We heaved a pumpkin from the bottom of the garden and set about the business of pie-making. We lived in a house in Islington with a long open-plan kitchen. I can't remember the pumpkin or the pie, but Mum tells me that when she came home with Jack there was a fine layer of flour over every single surface of the kitchen and dining room. No chair, table or shelf had escaped the flour bomb. I have no idea how we managed to create so much mess. Mum couldn't be cross – apparently Dad and I looked so pleased with ourselves that she couldn't help but laugh.

My earliest clear memory of Dad is when I was three years old in the kitchen of that house in Islington. It is raining outside and Dad is making sausage sandwiches, with crusty white bread and ketchup. I don't know where Mum is, but it is a rarity that Dad is looking after us. It is warm and cosy; all is well within my world.

Around this time Dad made *Mona Lisa* – the film widely considered to be one of his best. I find it strange to think of this. To me, Dad was just Dad, the man who made sausage sandwiches and took me to the park. It's hard to place the two figures – the man and the actor – together in my mind.

Directed by Neil Jordan and produced by Stephen Woolley, *Mona Lisa* tells the story of George, a naive ex-con who, upon release from prison, is given the job of driver and minder for a high-class prostitute, Simone (Cathy Tyson). George falls for Simone and agrees to help her find Cathy, an abused friend from her past. When they find her, George puts himself in grave danger to help both women and the film culminates in a violent confrontation. I visit Steve Woolley in his office in Soho to ask him about the making of the film.

Before *Mona Lisa*, Woolley and Jordan had made *A Company of Wolves* together. After production had finished, they discussed what they would do next. Steve drew Neil's attention to a story in the *News of the World* about a Maltese man who was being prosecuted for pimping. He was defended by two girls who said that he wasn't their pimp at all, that he had actually been protecting them from a violent criminal. At the same time, Paul Raymond – the owner of Raymond Revuebar in Soho – had gone public about some Maltese immigrants who were running peep shows and ripping people off by charging too much for champagne. The truth was slightly more complicated: Paul Raymond himself was charging extortionate rents and was running all the peep shows in Soho. In the Thatcher era, you could always buy respectability if you had enough money,

Steve tells me he wanted Dad for the part of George because he was a huge fan of his from *The Long Good Friday* and had seen him in *Guys and Dolls*. 'And I thought, Wow, this guy is fantastic! I also loved him because he came from north London, where I am also from.' To Steve, Dad was an actor from the streets – the genuine article. He thought George needed to be played by someone with a naivety, but a toughness too: 'Somebody who wouldn't be frightened, but who would also be sensitive and old-fashioned and might not always see what was going on around him.'

When Steve first talked to Neil Jordan about casting Dad, Neil had no idea who Dad was. Steve told him to watch *The Long Good Friday*. Neil watched it, and said he didn't think Dad was right for the part. Meanwhile Dad's agent, Sally Hope, had sent him the script, but he didn't like it. And besides, he had met someone in a pub who had offered him a part in a play where his entrance would be coming on stage with a huge fish. He liked that idea much more.

But Sally and Steve weren't to be deterred. 'I massaged Neil and forced him to meet Bob,' explains Steve, 'and she massaged Bob and forced him to meet Neil.' Neither man was aware of what was going on and it worked brilliantly. 'When we finally got them to go out and meet,' he says, 'it was great, because Bob could drink for England and Neil could drink for Ireland. After an hour, they'd fallen in love and were shaking hands and saying that working together was a great idea.'

For the part of Simone, the high-class call girl, they needed an actress who could convey sophisticated refinement and a savvy understanding of the sleazy underworld she moved through.

While the distributors were keen to use Grace Jones, Steve and Neil found the suggestion laughable. Steve says, 'Can you imagine Grace Jones – all six foot of her – and Bob Hoskins? That would have looked ridiculous.'

They auditioned Dad with Cathy Tyson, who was nineteen at the time and had never acted in a feature film. They knew they had found their girl. When I track Cathy down on social media, she invites me to her house and gives me a pot of tea and a plate of mince pies. Cathy remembers Dad being very kind to her on the day of the audition. But she was so convinced that she hadn't got the part that she left her script behind.

Previous to *Mona Lisa*, Cathy Tyson's only experience had been on stage in Liverpool. She had performed in *The Liverpool Blitz Show* and *The Tempest*, but that was all. She tells me she will always credit Dad with teaching her how to act. 'When I worked with him,' Cathy says, 'he was so good that I thought, Oh dear. But that's what acting is about – and should be about. It's about pain as well as elation.' She could see that Dad worked from the inside, could see his emotions working when she acted with him. 'That scene when he was crying on the pier was extraordinary. I remember my line was "Have you ever needed anybody?" and he just said, "All the time." I'd always presumed that it was difficult for men to cry but he just crumpled. It was very, very moving.'

Cathy was inexperienced and insecure. Steve and Cathy both tell me how Dad helped her during filming, how he was patient and generous with her. Steve remembers Dad always being courteous to everyone on set, but that he made a particular effort with Cathy: 'I think he realised that the strength of his part would be in believing her.'

Cathy admits she needed that support, because she was very lacking in confidence. 'If I did something wrong,' she says, 'he'd say to me, very gently, "Now try that again." Not in a horrible way; like a very patient teacher. And the next time I did it, it was better.' He didn't have any airs and graces, she recalls. He was humble and kind and she never heard anybody say a bad word against him. 'I'm very protective of that,' she adds.

When awards season came around, Dad's performance in the film earned him a BAFTA, a Golden Globe, a *Prix d'interprétation masculine* (Best Actor Award) at the Cannes Film Festival and an Oscar nomination.

I find writing about Dad difficult. I see him everywhere I look. Most of the furniture in my home is hand-me-downs from Mum and Dad. The table where I sit to write is the same one where we ate countless meals throughout my childhood. He's in the bones of my house – I sometimes fancy I catch a smell of him. Diving into his past life and work intensifies the grief. I'm not sure writing a book about him, so soon after he has died, is good for my mental health. But surrender is not an option.

I go to Mum's house and sort through a massive collection of family photos, stored in her attic. The boxes and boxes of snaps are relics of the days when photos were printed on shiny rectangles of paper.

I've often thought it a shame that Dad didn't live long enough to get his teeth into modern technology. When he travelled, he carted around books, CDs, DVDs, cameras, rolls of film and portable playing devices. He was rather nerdy and he'd have loved to load all his entertainment on to one or two slim gadgets. I bought him an iPad for Christmas in 2010, but he barely touched it. At the time, I was disappointed that he didn't seem to like it. In hindsight, it's clearly an early indication of his illness.

As I rummage through the thousands of photos, I find shots of Dad with Michael Caine, Denzel Washington, Alan Alda, Maggie Smith, Cher, Judi Dench. There's a vast heap of family photos: Dad obsessively documented our lives from the beginning. I think it was a relief for him to be behind the camera.

As I rifle through my life with Dad, I realise how lucky I am. Sometimes I forget there was a time before the illness took hold of him. I find a picture of the house we had in Sussex: it's a long, panoramic view of the landscape that Dad developed and printed himself.

I remember one warm summer's day when he came to pick me up from Lewes station. I got in his car. On the stereo he was playing a song called 'Daisy' by a folk singer called Karine Polwart. 'Listen to the lyrics of this, love,' he said, 'it's wonderful. Want a chewing gum? Give us one, will ya?' (He always had Wrigley's spearmint gum in the glove compartment of his car. To this day, the smell of car leather and mint reminds me of him.) We drove down the winding country roads, passing the bucolic scenery.

I grab my laptop now and search for 'Daisy' on Spotify. Within seconds I've clicked on the track. The spry melody transports me: I'm back in Dad's car, driving through the sunny countryside.

A few days later it's my first birthday without Dad.

I'm not in a mood to celebrate. We have all staggered through the past few weeks fuelled by shock and nervous energy.

In accordance with the example that Dad set his whole life, I am determined that today will not be a sad day. A group of my close friends, along with my husband Pete, Jack and Mum, go with me to have lunch in a pub. Although grief is bubbling away under the surface, we manage to have a fun afternoon.

When I get home, I arrange my birthday cards on the sideboard. I open the drawer underneath my display and find a stack of birthday cards from the last six years. (I'm not good at throwing things away.) I fish them out and flick through them. Mostly they're from people I don't know any more. Then I open one that stops me in my tracks. I recognise Dad's looping handwriting. This must be at least four years old. It's an Edward Monkton card with a poem on the front entitled 'The Beautiful Frock':

'Buy me, Lady,' said the frock, 'and I will make you into a BEAUTIFUL and WHOLE and COMPLETE Human Being.'

'Do not be SILLY,' said the Man, 'for a frock alone cannot do that.'

'TRUE,' said the Lady. 'I will have the Shoes and the Bag as well.'

Inside the card he'd written: 'Get it while it's going. Have the hat as well. Happy Birthday, love Dad XXX.'

If my memory serves me correctly, he was referring to a conversation we'd had a few days before my birthday about how eccentric I was when I was four years old. I never left the house without a hat. My favourite was my granddad's trilby, but I could be just as happy in a child-sized fireman's helmet, a croupier's visor or a baseball cap that Dad had been given on a film. I'd insist on wearing the cap with the peak to one side. We joked about what an oddball I was and Dad teased that nothing much had changed. He encouraged my idiosyncrasies from an early age. He loved how I was an eccentric little kid, and consequently a somewhat unconventional adult.

The card has reminded me of a conversation that I've forgotten all about, and I feel grateful for our relationship and the bond we shared.

CHAPTER SEVEN

WHEN *MONA LISA* WENT to Cannes, no one really thought the film, or Dad, would win anything. Dad flew home. Steve Woolley and Neil Jordan stayed for the award ceremony. Steve was lying on the public beach on the Saturday when he got a call to say that they needed to get Dad back over, as it looked as though he was going to win the *Prix d'interprétation masculine* (Best Actor Award). Back in England, Dad was pruning the roses in the garden with Mum. He received a call telling him he needed to get on a plane. He and Mum had to move fast. My grandparents stepped in to babysit and my folks threw a few clothes in a bag. A private jet was laid on to get them to Cannes quickly, and they were given a police escort from the airport to the ceremony at the other end.

The ceremony was in full flow while they were en route, but they couldn't give Dad his award until he arrived. 'The ceremony organisers kept calling him La Bob,' remembers Steve Woolley. '"La Bob is on his way." "La Bob is at the airport." The audience were being given a running commentary so, when he finally arrived, the whole place went nuts. "La Bob!"'

As well as the Best Actor at Cannes, Dad also won a BAFTA and a Golden Globe. The Golden Globes was a great night: *Mona Lisa* had six nominations, including Dad for Best Actor and Cathy Tyson for Best Actress. But in the end Dad was the only winner. The same happened at the BAFTAs – six nominations but only one won, by Dad. 'He thoroughly deserved it,' says Steve. 'He got robbed of the Oscar that year because it was Paul Newman's turn for the sympathy vote.'

Dad was very funny about his missed Oscars opportunity. 'Tattiest do I'd ever been to in my life,' he'd often say. 'I went downstairs to the bar and there were my fellow nominees – James Woods, Dexter Gordon, William Hurt. They said, "Sit down, Bob. Here's to Paul Newman." And I said, "What are you talking about? I'm going to win this." And James said, "Listen, have I given an Oscar-winning performance?" and I said, "Yes." "And has he? Has he?" (indicating Gordon and Hurt) and I said, "Yes." And he said, "And has Paul Newman for *The Colour of Money*?" And I said, "No, he hasn't." And he said, "Well, here's to Paul Newman then." And by the time Newman won it, we'd all been in the bar long enough that we were in hysterics.'

As I've said earlier, Dad didn't think much of awards. Of course, he and Mum enjoyed the glitz and the glamour of the business from time to time. Over the years they socialised with Michael Caine, Liza Minnelli, Bob Dylan and Sammy Davis Jr, to name but a few.

But mostly they preferred a quiet home life, cooking a tasty dinner and enjoying a glass of wine. They knew that much of the business is hollow and vacuous. Dad could work the room better than anyone if he had to – he was charming and funny, the life and soul of any party.

But once in a while he grew frustrated by the pretention. After one black-tie party, Dad was particularly disgruntled and decided he never wanted to attend that kind of event again. Mum and Dad arrived home, where Polly Hill, Dave and Jane's daughter, was babysitting. Dad shook off his tuxedo jacket, grabbed a pair of kitchen scissors and cut the jacket in half.

To be fair, cutting up his jacket wasn't the sort of thing he did regularly. In fact, I don't ever remember him behaving like that when I was around. That said, he could sometimes be over-bearing. My parents didn't argue often but, when they did, Dad would shout the house down. But Mum could hold her own.

I remember overhearing one row when Dad hollered, 'I am an artist!'

Which Mum swiftly deflated with, 'Yes. You are also an idiot!'

I was very proud of Mum in that moment. Anyone who proclaims to be an artist is basically saying, 'I am a child but I demand to be treated like a king!' I should know: I've done it more times than I care to admit.

•••

I could be an impish child, particularly when Dad was away working. Although he tried to coordinate his work to coincide with the school holidays, it was not always possible and there were many times when he was away for long periods. I'm sure all children dislike the absence of a parent and I was no exception to the rule.

My mum was essentially a single mother during those periods, and it must have been tough for her. When Dad was home, he wasn't a strict disciplinarian, except when we overstepped the line. Dad wouldn't need to say much: we knew that if we were really out of order he'd lose his temper. He'd let loose an almighty roar that terrified both Jack and me. But he was all bark and no bite – he would get angry, shout for a few seconds, and then the telling-off would be over in a flash. My mother's scolding of us was more frequent and reasonable, and less scary.

If Jack and I really acted up when Dad was away, Mum would pick up the phone as a threat: 'If you don't behave, I'm going to call your father.' It was a seldom-used and rather toothless threat – after all, what was he going to do from the other side of the world? However, the very suggestion made us promise to be good. Once or twice she did call him and put us on the phone. His gruff voice, growling out of the handset, was enough to make me stop whatever naughty behaviour I'd been indulging in – usually fighting with Jack – and I'd toe the line.

Looking back, I realise that my mischief-making was just a way of making up for Dad's absences. The usual target of these larks was Ray Ward. Ray is very similar to Dad in build and, to some extent, in his manner. He's also a born-and-bred north Londoner.

Ray first came into our lives when I was around five years old. He was doing a bit of painting and decorating in the house in Islington. One day when Dad was away a pigeon got into the house. The frenzied bird flapped up and down the long kitchen and Mum didn't know what to do, so she called Ray.

He was only around the corner, he remembers, so he went straight round to the house and got rid of the pigeon. He says, 'There were times when it was handy to have a fella around who could help out, if Linda needed it.' Ray was only going back to working part-time when Dad phoned him up one day and said, 'I want to talk to you – where are you comfortable?' They met in Ray's local pub and Dad said, 'I want you to work for me full-time.' So Ray started to work full-time driving for Dad. His job includes gardening, maintaining the house, and generally sorting out anything that needs doing. He's like an uncle to me.

Ray describes my five-year-old self as a 'tormentor': 'I used to laugh because you didn't just used to torment Jack, you tormented the life out of me.' I'd unplug the Hoover, hide the paint brushes – anything I could do to cause aggravation. Ray supposes it was because I'd normally lark around with my dad. And when he wasn't there to do that with, it was handy to have another man around.

When Dad came home once, he caught me playing the switching-off-the-Hoover trick on Ray and thought it was hilarious, so then poor Ray had to put up with it from Dad as well. When the gardener came to mow the lawn, he would plug the mower into the socket in Dad's office downstairs. Dad and Ray then started turning off the switch and leaving the poor gardener in the middle of the lawn, scratching his head.

Dad was great at having fun. If we children ever went on a rollercoaster, he would come too, happy with the excuse that we needed to have adult supervision.

And it wasn't just rollercoasters. Dad was good at entertaining us kids. I remember the way he used to read me a version of 'The Three Little Pigs' called 'The Three Little Pigs by A. Wolf'. It's a retelling of the tale from the wolf's point of view. Dad would narrate the beleaguered wolf in an Al Capone voice.

He came close to playing Capone in Brian De Palma's *The Untouchables*. De Palma offered the part to Dad, but eventually Robert De Niro, who had been De Palma's first choice, was cast instead. A few months later a cheque arrived from Brian De Palma for $200,000. 'I phoned him up,' Dad would say, 'and

I said, "Brian, if you've ever got any other films you don't want me to be in, son, you just give me a call."'

Had the opportunity come his way Dad would have taken the role, but the truth is he didn't want to be pigeonholed as a gangster. *The Long Good Friday* and *Mona Lisa* had been good for his career, but he didn't want to get stuck playing the stereo-typical 'hard man'.

However, the role of Harold Shand had affected the way people viewed him. Dave Hill tells a story of when he was hav-ing a bit of trouble from the landlord of the pub next door to where he lived. He asked Dad to come down to the pub with him – not to say anything, but just to stand next to Dave.

With Dad beside him, Dave said to the landlord, 'I've come down to sort this all out once and for all.'

The landlord looked at Dad, then he looked at Dave, and he said, 'No, don't worry. Everything will be all right.'

I find letters to Dad from Ronnie Kray, tucked away in the family archive. He wrote them from prison. The writing is mostly indecipherable, but I can make out the phrase 'From your friend, Ronnie Kray'.

When he was talked about in the press, Dad was often referred to as 'hard man Bob Hoskins'. He could sometimes slip into playing the role of 'Bob Hoskins'. He'd play up the cockney charm and give talk-show hosts and journalists what they expected. He was tough; he had come from a background where you had to be. But underneath his outer shell, the reality was rather different.

After *Mona Lisa*, Dad's career moved in a new direction. He made a film with Maggie Smith, directed by Jack Clayton, called *The Lonely Passion of Judith Hearne*, about an Irish spinster who falls in love with a duplicitous hotel entrepreneur. The result won both Maggie and Dad *Evening Standard* Film Awards.

Soon after, Dad received a call from Robert Zemeckis, inviting him to audition for another of his career-defining roles.

CHAPTER EIGHT

GOING THROUGH DAD'S THINGS, I come across a photograph, rolled up in a cardboard tube. It's a still from *Who Framed Roger Rabbit*. A large image of Eddie Valiant and Roger Rabbit handcuffed together. I spread it out on the table and examine it closely; this is a version of Dad that I remember from my childhood.

When I was small I had several invisible friends. My favourite was a boy called Geoffrey. Geoffrey and I played all the time, wrapped up in my own little fantasy world. I don't remember very much about him, but Dad used to play with us both for hours in order to teach himself how to hallucinate for the role of Eddie Valiant in *Who Framed Roger Rabbit*.

Dad often talked about how Geoffrey and I helped him prepare for the role. 'I always managed to sit on Geoffrey,' he said, 'which you complained about a lot. That's when I realised that, as a kid, your imagination is so close to the front of your head. It's part of your reality. So, when I knew I'd got the job, I spent hours and hours playing with you, pushing my own imagination to the front of my head. Eventually I could do it.

Eventually I could hallucinate. Which was the only way I felt I could play the part.'

During Dad's preparation for *Roger Rabbit* he was sent a huge box of cartoons on video. He, Jack and I watched television for days on end, totally absorbed.

Who Framed Roger Rabbit is set in a fantasy version of 1940s Hollywood, where cartoons and humans interact. Eddie Valiant is a private detective who is hired to investigate a crime being pinned on a cartoon comedian called Roger Rabbit. Filming began at Elstree Studios on 2 December 1986 and lasted for seven months. After that there was an additional month's filming in Los Angeles.

Robert Zemeckis kindly agrees to be interviewed about his time working with Dad. Initially I'm excited to have an excuse to visit California, but it soon becomes obvious that flying all the way there for one hour-long interview isn't exactly practical. We rearrange to talk on the phone. I'm not nervous about speaking to Mr Zemeckis: I have questions prepared and I watched *Who Framed Roger Rabbit* earlier in the week.

I dial the number and a West Coast accent answers the phone. 'Bob Zemeckis's office?'

An unexpected ball of nerves rises in my throat.

'Oh, hello, it's Rosa Hoskins here. I have an appointment to speak to Mr Zemeckis.'

Robert Zemeckis's jovial voice crackles out of my

mobile – the line isn't good. I have set up the recording device next to the phone and have my computer on my lap, ready to take notes. The line continues to whir and buzz. I am anxious the recording will be unintelligible. My fingers sprint over the keyboard, trying to apply a clumsy shorthand and preserve Robert's words. As my nerves escalate, my kitten Cleo attacks my fingers like a lioness hunting zebra on the Serengeti. She leaps upon the keyboard and engages in a death wrestle with my left hand. I shoo away the bloodthirsty kitten just as Robert Zemeckis finishes the answer to my first question. I have lost my train of thought. The computer screen swims out of focus and the phone line hisses. An awkward moment of silence while I grope for the next question.

'Oh, well, that's very interesting. I, um, hadn't thought of it, um, like that . . .'

I trail off and feel a livid blush rising in my cheeks. I find the next question and the conversation hobbles on like a three-legged donkey. Robert Zemeckis is patient and kind, probably sensing my nerves. It's always preferable to conduct an interview face to face: you can read a person's body language and establish a friendly interaction. Over the phone it's difficult to manufacture repartee with a stranger. Despite my incompetent interview technique, Robert shares some interesting insights about the making of *Who Framed Roger Rabbit*.

He tells me that Dad wasn't the first choice for the role. 'To be perfectly honest,' he says, 'I wanted Paul Newman, but he was quite insulted that I had even sent him the script.' Then Jeffrey Katzenberg, an executive at Disney, said to him, 'It's ridiculous to put a giant star in this movie. What you really need is a great actor.' After screen-testing several other actors, Robert met Dad in his London office. He thought Dad was able to create the illusion of talking to someone who's not there better than anyone else. 'Also, he just looked like he belonged in the 1940s in that shabby suit. Without his performance, the movie just wouldn't have worked. If there were ever a definition of the word "natural", it was Bob.'

Robert's favourite moment in the film is when Eddie and Roger are on the theatre balcony and Eddie tells Roger his story. He says to me that he did that scene with no editing. It was one long elaborate shot that starts with Eddie and the rabbit and then pushes in on Eddie. Dad had shown up to work that day with a burst blood vessel in his eye – it was completely red. 'If you look closely,' Robert says, 'you'll see what I'm talking about. But there was nothing I could do. I couldn't not shoot. And the end result was amazing.'

When I was a kid, I found the plot of *Who Framed Roger Rabbit* confusing. I didn't understand the conspiracy and the corruption.

I also found it frightening. The scene in a bar where Eddie shoves an egg into a man's mouth was particularly disturbing for me. I remember going to a screening of the film and being so frightened that Mum had to take Jack and me out of the cinema. My parents thought I had got my head around the concept that Dad was an actor and that what was on the screen wasn't real, but I obviously hadn't.

A little while after watching *Roger Rabbit*, we were sitting at dinner and I asked, 'Daddy, what was it like when you drove into Toon Town?' While I had understood that it was make-believe, I hadn't figured out that Toon Town was not another location on the film. When I was older, I watched it again and loved it. This was when I realised Dad's job was different from my friends' parents' jobs.

As the years wore on, I avoided telling new people that I had a famous parent straight away. I wanted to be judged on my character rather than on my proximity to fame. Reactions from other kids varied. Often they would be excited, asking how many famous people I'd met, what they were like and so on. Sometimes they became more interested in striking up a friendship with a famous actor's daughter. A few responded with hostility, assuming that I thought I was better than them because my dad was famous. It affected me to a certain extent, but I didn't waste much effort fretting about it. If anything, I found it tiresome: there was an extra social barrier that had to be scaled before I could begin to build genuine relationships. I became adept at sniffing out disingenuous advances from potential friends.

When I started university, I kept it very quiet for the first few weeks of term. The first person I told was my friend Alice, with whom I'm still very close. We were sitting in a sunny courtyard on campus when she asked me the direct question 'What do your parents do?'

I answered honestly and she promised to be discreet.

Once I got to know a few other people, I opened up and it quickly spread around the campus. There was one occasion when I met a music student called Andy – a few of us were in the common room in the hall of residence. He asked what course we were on. When we told him drama, he said, 'Have you heard that Bob Hoskins's daughter is on the drama course?'

'Yeah,' I replied, 'that's me.'

We all laughed.

As a small child, I enjoyed visiting Dad at work, but going to the *Roger Rabbit* set was overwhelming. The scenes in the Acme factory were shot in the Dimco buildings in Shepherd's Bush. I remember walking into the cavernous space and feeling dwarfed by the massive set and filming equipment.

When I watch the film now, I have a fresh understanding of why it works. Although the world of the film is exaggerated and stylised, there is a damaged man at its centre, which gives it weight and substance.

Charles Fleischer, who provided the voice for Roger, was there every day, speaking Roger's lines and performing opposite Dad off camera. He even insisted on dressing in a rabbit costume while on set. The production of the film was intricate and complicated. During the rehearsals on set, rubber mannequins of the cartoons were used to help the actors know where to look when acting opposite fresh air. When it came to doing a take, the actors would perform without them. It took incredible focus and technical skill. Many of the live-action props held by cartoon characters were shot on set either with robotic arms holding them or manipulated by strings, like puppets.

Robert Zemeckis thinks Dad's performance worked because he really believed the cartoon characters were there in front of him. 'I'd just say to him, "You know, Bob, the rabbit is three feet away. You have to look at it rather than through it. If you focus on your finger a foot away, you can't look at a point on the wall because it doesn't work. You have to be able to go slightly cross-eyed for it to work." And you know what? He could just do it. We never had to struggle.'

Dad was short-sighted, and he never wore contact lenses.

(He didn't like anyone touching his eyes.) His poor eyesight might have been useful in this situation, as it's easier to focus on an imaginary figure when your eyes are a little bit blurry anyway.

A lot of money had been poured into the project – $50 million, the equivalent of $250 million today. Everyone was really stressed on the film. In film terms, they were doing a high-wire act with no safety net and were all fearful that the whole thing would be a disaster. No one had ever tried anything so bizarre. Robert says, 'The only movies that were tried were really horrible movies like *Pete's Dragon*. Or little dance routines like in *Mary Poppins*.' There had never been a film that was like a 1940s film noir but with cartoon characters. 'It was beyond insane. No one thought it would ever work for one second, so we were all working our hearts out. I remember feeling constant terror.'

The stress of the production took its toll on Dad. One Monday morning he went into work, grabbed Robert Zemeckis and said, 'I'm losing my fucking mind! I'm seeing weasels all over the place. I'm sitting at home, having dinner with my wife and my mother-in-law, and this fucking weasel comes in and puts its dick in my ear! I'm losing my fucking mind, I tell you.'

One of his most difficult scenes to shoot was when the weasels hang Eddie Valiant out of a window. Dad was high up on a harness and strung up with cables, remembers Robert. 'And everything on this movie took for ever. Poor Bob was hanging upside down for hours and hours.' When they finally got the shot and let him down, his entire body was trembling from head to toe.

Robert had never seen anything like it. 'Jesus, Bob, what's wrong?' he asked.

Dad admitted he was terrified of heights.

'Why didn't you tell me?' said Robert.

And Dad said, 'Well, we needed to get the shot, didn't we?'

Everyone I speak to about him talks about Dad's rigorous work ethic. ('You know what his famous saying was, don't you?' says Ray Winstone: '"Are we making a film here or are we fucking about?"') 'He never once complained. Ever,' says Robert Zemeckis. 'Never any animosity, or anything that was negative. Even when we had him up on wires for hours, acting being thrown around by a gorilla.'

When Dad came home from a job, he regularly talked about how much he liked the crew. He loved the camaraderie of being part of a company. Robert thinks this was helpful on the set of *Roger Rabbit*, because if a crew sees an actor working hard, they work even harder. There are actors who can't come out of their trailer for an hour, who're not in wardrobe when they need to be, and the crew are busting their backsides to

Nanny was very proud of Dad from an early age. She entered this photo into a baby competition and they won. I think Dad's quiff impressed the judges.

Dad's around two in this shot. Nanny would have knitted him this little cardigan.

This is from a family holiday to the seaside when Dad was about 10. He looks like he's about to launch into a speech from *Henry V*, 'Once more unto the breach dear friends!'

Dad is about 17 in this shot with his cousins. Goodness knows what they're doing with a sheep.

ABOVE LEFT:
I can't pass Tower Bridge without thinking of this scene from *The Long Good Friday*.

BELOW LEFT:
I love this picture of Dad from *Pennies From Heaven*, it shows some of his exuberance and energy.

RIGHT AND BELOW:
My parents' wedding day.

RIGHT: Mum took this photo when we were living in New York. Dad and I were like two stocky little peas in a pod.

BELOW: Jack is around 4 months old; I think Dad enjoyed being a father.

I was a jolly baby and Dad found me very funny. I'm sure I thought he was hilarious too.

ABOVE: We are in Australia visiting a park with emus and wallabies. I was trying to hug the animals, hence the reins. Note Dad's sophisticated 'Brits abroad' head gear.

RIGHT: The burly snowman Dad and I made in the garden of our house in Islington.

ABOVE: While Dad was filming *Hook*, we lived in LA in a house with a weird black pool. Jack and I used to grab onto a shoulder each and Dad would swim the length of the pool, like an orca whale with us on his back.

Dad and Cathy Tyson in my favourite scene from *Mona Lisa*.

It's easy to forget that he was acting against thin air in *Who Framed Roger Rabbit*.

ABOVE: Dad in LA with David Crosby and Jim Hart. The Hart family are dear friends and we see them whenever they come to London.

LEFT: Dad and Robin Williams got on very well. Dad appears to be holding a flower by his ear, I'm not sure why.

Our wedding was one of the happiest days of my life. I'm so glad we got married before Dad became ill.

light a set when the actor can't even remember their lines. It can be demoralising for a crew. 'A lot of actors have that selfish streak in them,' Robert says. 'But not Bob. He was helpful and he would work as hard as the crew, if not harder, to get the best end result. I can't tell you what a difference this made to me.' Robert was working with a British crew for the first time and, before he started, people had cautioned him, telling him how tough crews in Britain could be, voting on whether to let the director work them into overtime. 'But on *Roger Rabbit* they didn't ever say no. Not once. And that was all because of your dad.'

Two weeks after filming had started, *Who Framed Roger Rabbit* wrapped for Christmas and started up again at Elstree Studios just after New Year. At Elstree, there were two bars: the 'above the line' bar, for executives, and the 'below the line' bar for crew. Dad always drank in the below-the-line bar with the crew. He never went up with the directors or producers.

At the end of the first day of shooting at Elstree, Zemeckis called, 'That's a wrap.'

Dad approached him with a gigantic grin on his face. 'We've got to go and have a drink,' he said, and took Robert to the bar. 'They love you,' he told him. 'The crew loves you!' Then he admitted that he had been concerned that they would eat Zemeckis alive.

I interview a variety of people who represent a wide

demographic of the business. Everyone has something similar to say about Dad: he worked hard and understood that making a film is a collaborative process. A lot of actors behave poorly on set – partly because they can, but mostly due to their insecurities. Dad never brought hang-ups to work, primarily because he had so few.

Talking to Dad's colleagues has been poignant, but I feel lucky to find out more about him. Their stories keep his memory close to me.

There was one job that generated some wonderful stories, although it's one of Dad's lesser-known films. Between *Mona Lisa* and *Who Framed Roger Rabbit*, he made a film called *The Raggedy Rawney*, which was filmed in Czechoslovakia. We went to visit him in Prague. I have a distinct memory of climbing into a massive fountain and splashing around in the water. I now know it was Křižík's Fountain, a rather grand structure built in 1891. At the time I thought of it as a giant paddling pool. I don't know what the rules are around the fountain now, but I don't remember there being any official who told my parents off for letting me leap into the water.

Dad co-wrote the script of *The Raggedy Rawney* with Nicole de Wilde, as well as directing and starring in the film. George Harrison and HandMade Films financed the project.

It's set in war-torn eastern Europe and tells the story of Tom, played by Dexter Fletcher, an army recruit who deserts his troop during an artillery barrage. He's a traumatised fugitive and takes shelter with a travelling Gypsy caravan, led by Darky (played by Dad). Tom disguises himself as a 'Rawney', a magical madwoman who can control animals and see the future. He becomes romantically involved with Darky's daughter Jessie, and gets her pregnant. She was played by Zoë Nathenson, who had also played Dad's daughter in *Mona Lisa*.

Dad cast his friends in the parts. Dave Hill, Jane Wood, Gawn Grainger, Jim Carter and Zoë Wanamaker all starred alongside him. As well as jumping in that fountain, I remember there being a jolly atmosphere in the hotel, what with it being populated by Dad's convivial actor mates.

Dexter Fletcher had worked with Dad on *The Long Good Friday* when he was a boy. 'I was the cheeky little blighter,' says Dexter. 'There was the classic line "from little acorns grow mighty oaks", but I'd met Bob before that.' It was at a party thrown by theatre director Dusty Hughes when Dexter was about eleven. Dad was there and Dexter recognised him as the guy from *On the Move*, which he remembers watching when he didn't have to go to school.

Dad and Zoë Nathenson had become close since making *Mona Lisa*. Dad called everyone and invited them for dinner. He said, 'Right. I've been asked to do this film, *The Raggedy*

Rawney.' He'd sat down one night with producer Bob Weiss, over a few drinks. 'And much like your dad would do,' says Dexter, 'he'd come up with stories, ideas. You got him in the right mood and he'd be on a roll. This bloke's gone and written up the idea, and it's *The Raggedy Rawney.* I don't remember ever auditioning for it or anything like that, he just gave me the part.'

When I was a teenager, I asked Dad if the story of *The Raggedy Rawney* was based on our vague Gypsy heritage.

He said, 'No, love, it was just something I dreamed up once.'

When he was alive I didn't much analyse Dad's imagination. It's only now that I understand how unusual he was in that respect. Zoë Wanamaker had worked with Dad a few years earlier at the Royal Shakespeare Company. She views Dad's ability to create myths as one of the most wonderful things about him. She could never quite be sure if he'd made a story up or not because it would be so fantastical. When they were making *The Raggedy Rawney* he would talk about mystical stuff that would come to him, and to Zoë it would seem very spiritual. 'I'm very down to earth,' she says, 'and I would love to have things – spiritual things – happen to me, but it never happens. Bob just took off on to that level sometimes, and me the cynic would step back from it, because I never believed half of what he said was true. But that part of it didn't matter,' she admits, 'because that was the joy of him. The joy of him was knowing he was that close to levitating and that his imaginary life, however fantastical it was, was very deep and very strong and spiritual.'

And if some of his stories were exaggerated or untrue, it didn't matter. The stories became real to him and when he told them they were incredibly vivid.

In a move typical of his generosity, he gave work to his friends, and to friends of friends. Dexter tells me that Dad cast his two brothers in the film, as well as their flatmate Perry Fenwick. Zoë Nathenson got a part for her best friend, Melissa Wilkes, who'd been in *Grange Hill* and who Dad thought was great. Lois Burwell, an old friend of Dad's, was the make-up designer. 'But that's what you do when you get your first film up and running,' Dexter explains. 'It was his first film and it's always difficult, you've got to play the game, play the role. But that's how smart he was – to surround himself with people who he knew and understood him, who he could already communicate with and you know are very good and do what you want them to do.'

Although the cast and crew had fun on *The Raggedy Rawney*, it was a very stressful job for Dad. He used to say that he never wanted to be 'lumbered' with directing. I think he found being in charge of the whole operation vexing.

Dexter was nervous to be directed by Dad – something he's discovering for himself now that he too is a director. He tells me that it's difficult to communicate with actors when you yourself are one: the director may think he knows what the straight direct line is, but actually it can be more complex than he realises because each actor's approach is different. So what the director thinks is a straightforward way of telling someone what he wants them to do, what he needs from them, can sometimes undo what the actor has done themselves. 'Not to say that your dad did that with me,' he adds, 'but thinking back on it, if I'm honest, I don't know if we had amazing communication.' Dexter thinks part of the problem was that Dad was surrounded by a group of very experienced actors who were also his friends, who all knew exactly what they were doing. 'Because when I look at it now,' he says, 'I don't think I did a particularly good job of it. That's my own subjective opinion.'

The first scene they shot had Dexter, as Tom, lying in a river. It's the first time he meets Dad's character, Darky. Dad told him, 'I want pain, anguish, happiness, joy, fear.' An entire list of emotions that Dexter had to portray in the scene, but he had absolutely no lines. 'The trouble was,' he tells me, 'that the cheeky, lively kid that I was, that he first met at twelve or thirteen, was no longer around.' Dexter had become an awkward teenager who didn't know the first thing about acting, as far as Dad was concerned. 'And I think your dad thought, What the fuck's happened to him? He just wanted me to be able to deliver that. There's nothing wrong with that, but he didn't know how to access it in me, I don't think. I think there was an element of frustration with me from him. Not that I ever felt that, it's only in hindsight – he didn't explode at me or anything like that.'

I can understand where Dexter is coming from. Although Dad was usually very patient and nurturing with younger actors who he was playing opposite, when he was directing and had to deal with all the other demands of the film he wouldn't have had time to support Dexter.

It's funny how life turns out sometimes. Zoë Nathenson quit acting and started her own agency, and she is now my agent.

On the set, Zoë asked Dad, 'Are you going to direct me?'

'No,' he said, 'I'll tell you if you get it wrong, but you know what you're doing.'

He just let them get on with it.

Zoë believes Dad struggled to balance being a director with acting. There was one scene with a long shot on a Steadicam. He had forgotten he was in the very last bit of the shot. They were standing by the monitors, as it was being filmed. 'I'm good in this bit,' Dad said to Zoë. Then, 'Oh fuck!' as he went tearing off to get in shot.

'But the freedom he gave us was lovely,' she recalls. 'I think it's because he surrounded himself with people who were like family to him, so he had faith in us to go forth. But he was nervous to do it and he never wanted to direct again. Afterwards, he had a new respect for how hard the director has to work.'

There were other things that stressed Dad out on *The Raggedy Rawney*, not least singer Ian Dury, who played a small part in the film. Dad always spoke very fondly of Dury, but he caused quite a ruckus during the production.

Dexter Fletcher tells me how Ian Dury would go down to the hotel reception and order six prostitutes. (This was in Prague, and prostitutes would simply wander around in the lobby. It was the only Western hotel in the whole Eastern Bloc.) Dad said to Dexter, 'Dury's got all these women up in his room. What am I gonna do? I've got to buy them all off because he doesn't wanna fuck them. I've got to get up in the morning and direct a film!'

Dury would also shout at German people – 'You fucking Nazis!' – and he'd get really dark. The rest of the cast didn't witness much of it, but Dad would tell them about it the next day. But then Ian Dury would show moments of kindness too. They were filming a night shoot with things exploding, and Dexter was freezing. Dury took Dexter's hands and placed them under his arms, telling him, 'It's the only way to keep your hands warm.'

Zoë Nathenson also remembers the potential trouble that

Ian Dury could have landed Dad in. When they'd first arrived at the airport in Prague – still Communist at the time – the place had looked like a prison. As they all approached passport control, Dury said to Dad, 'Here, I've got some really good gear on me. We're going to have a great time!'

Dad looked at him. 'You've fucking brought drugs with you!' he said. 'Are you fucking crazy? Throw them out the window.' So Spider, Ian Dury's minder, had to go over to a window with bars on it and try to chuck the drugs out.

As I said, Dad always spoke kindly of Ian Dury, but I think he found him a bit of a handful. All of this came on top of the fact that Dad was still filming pick-ups for *Who Framed Roger Rabbit*, and he was hallucinating marauding weasels.

CHAPTER NINE

BEING THE CHILD OF an actor had its drawbacks – we would miss Dad terribly whenever he was away – but there were some fun bonuses too. When I was growing up I had some experiences that most children never get to have. One of those, which will stay with me for ever, was the time in 1991 when Jack and I were taken out of school so we could all go to Los Angeles for three months. Dad was filming *Hook*, Steven Spielberg's story of Peter Pan after he has grown up. Peter Pan (Robin Williams) is a boring lawyer who has forgotten all about who he once was. But when Captain Hook (Dustin Hoffman) kidnaps Peter's children in order to exact revenge on him, he is taken back to his magical past. Dad played Captain Hook's first mate, Smee. After *Pirates of the Caribbean*, *Hook* is the most successful pirate film of all time.

It was the only time Jack and I were taken out of school to go with Dad on a job. We lived in a villa on Doheny Drive in Beverly Hills, which had a strange black swimming pool in the garden, as was the fashion in the early nineties. To my memory, the house had a massive kitchen with a panoramic view over the city. Mum has since told me that the house was actually pretty modest in comparison to the grand mansions that surrounded us. But to a child the place felt vast.

For the duration of our time in LA, Mum home-schooled us. There was a strict routine. We woke early and had lessons that followed the curriculum being taught back home. Mum's background as a teacher served us well: by the time we got back to school, the levels that Jack and I were performing at had been considerably raised. I was very dyslexic and the teachers at my school, King Alfred, had voiced concerns that taking me out for such a long time would be unfavourable to my development. However, after three months of one-to-one tuition with my mum, my reading ability improved and my scruffy handwriting was much more legible.

After our morning lessons, we'd swim for hours in the black pool. We were energetic, rough-and-tumble kids and we needed to blow off plenty of steam. At the time, Jack and I were obsessed with Disney's *The Jungle Book* and *The Little Mermaid*. We'd spend hours and hours playing at being monkeys, bears and mermaids and continually sang Disney songs, which must have been a treat for our parents.

Every evening after filming, Dad would come home and we'd all have dinner together. We loved having a father who came home after work.

The Neverland set was inside Sony Studios in Culver City

and had taken six months to build. It was huge and spread out over several sound stages. There was a full-scale pirate ship and an elaborate pirate town, which had my brother and me wide-eyed with delight. Of course, it was a working set so we weren't given free run of the place, but that didn't matter to us. Everything was designed in such intricate detail that wherever we looked, there was some extraordinary sight or other, like a twenty-foot-high crocodile with a huge clock in its mouth. For a seven-year-old child, it was a magical, awe-inspiring place.

One day that especially sticks in my mind is when we were heading into the building to visit Dad and walked on to the sound stage just as some pirate extras had finished filming for the day. Mum, Jack and I were being led upstairs by a runner when a troupe of pirates came stomping down the stairs. The production team had recruited LA's biker community to play the pirate extras. They were gnarled and scarred and many of them were missing limbs – their appearance was startling to say the least. We stood in awe at the bottom of the stairs as these barbarous-looking men filed past us. Despite appearances, they were all very kind. Jack, who was five at the time, was clutching his favourite Spider-Man action figure and many of them commented on what a cool toy he had. Once the last of them had hobbled away, we made our way up the stairs to see Dad.

Often we would have to sit in Dad's trailer before he showed up in his pirate's costume. When he finally came in, he would say "Ello, my sweethearts!' in such a massive, booming voice that it would shake every fixture in the Winnebago. The swashbuckling atmosphere of the set seemed to make everyone in the cast very jovial; at least it appeared so from my child's perspective. Everyone would laugh and joke and say things like 'Aye, aye, me hearties!' a lot.

Very often a pirate friend would come knocking on the door of Dad's trailer. One I remember particularly well was David Crosby of Crosby, Stills and Nash. In his costume he looked more like a Viking than a pirate, but he had that raucous *joie de vivre* that was a prerequisite for a Hollywood pirate.

The film had caused such a buzz that all manner of celebrities were clamouring for a cameo. Glenn Close was another unlikely pirate. She wore a beard and a wig and played the unfortunate crew member that Hook places in the boo box, a chest with a hatch at the top through which live scorpions are fed. Dad told me that he had heard a rumour that Michael Jackson wanted to be a pirate, but Steven Spielberg hadn't wanted too many celebrity extras distracting from the story.

Jack and I weren't interested in famous people – we were much more concerned with where our next sugar hit would come from. Dad's trailer was well stocked with big glass bowls of gummy bears and chocolate M&Ms. I'm not sure if they had been put there for Dad's benefit, or if he had asked for them to be filled up because his family was visiting that day. Predictably, it ended in tears: two overexcited children hyped up on sugar and E numbers in a confined space is always going to be a recipe for disaster. In hindsight I feel sorry for Mum, who must have had to mop up the debris after we had come down from the sugar rush. The next time we visited, the bowls of sweets were conspicuous by their absence.

Robin Williams, who played the grown-up Peter Pan, was one of the loveliest men I have ever met, very kind and attentive. Robin was similar to Dad. Both of them had the ability to connect with the mindset of a child. At one Sunday get-together he played with Jack and me in the pool for hours. He hadn't anticipated how boisterous my brother and I were. We insisted on riding on his back as though he were an orca whale at Sea-World. The poor man eventually came spluttering to the surface, gasping for air. He later told Dad that we were great kids but that we'd nearly drowned him.

During our time in LA we went to all kinds of exciting places, like Disneyland and the fairground on Santa Monica Pier. One of my strongest memories is of sitting on a bench with Dad at Disneyland, eating hot churros and watching the world go by. Memory works in strange ways. Rollercoasters and Disney never remind me of Los Angeles and *Hook*, but if I catch a whiff of hot sugar and cinnamon I am instantly transported back to being a seven-year-old in Hollywood with my dad.

Looking back, I have come to understand how difficult it must have been for Mum to raise two kids on her own half of the time. Trips like that one to visit Dad in LA were rare. Mum and Dad hired a nanny to support her, and my grandparents lived close by. Nonetheless, it must have been challenging to hold the fort whenever he was away.

Dad often claimed that he owed a lot of his success to my mum. 'Not everyone has a Linda,' he would say.

By this he meant that she could manage money and run a household better than anyone. She created a stable home that not only allowed Jack and me to thrive, but was beneficial for him as well. He wasn't able to create stability for himself. He had talent and a creative flair, but he was no good at dotting the i's and crossing the t's of life. After he married Mum he grew calmer and more settled.

If Mum hadn't managed the family coffers, Dad would have blown the lot. In his younger days he would give out wads of cash to beggars in the street and be the first to buy everyone a round of drinks at the bar, even when he could barely afford one for himself, as in the days of the Ken Campbell Roadshow.

He grew more sensible with age. However, his core generosity certainly never withered.

Sammy Pasha, Dad's long-time minder and stand-in in over sixty films, remembers this side of him with fondness: 'If you said, "Oh, I'm hungry," he'd give you his dinner. He'd say, "You eat that – I'll eat later." Most people would buy you a sandwich or something, but he would actually give you the food off his own plate. He was a very unusual man in that respect.'

Sometimes Dad's generosity could be a touch disconcerting. When I was a student at Middlesex University, studying drama, there was a month or so when a serial rapist was attacking young women in the neighbourhood where my housemates and I lived. Dad was understandably alarmed at the thought of someone attacking me or one of my friends. When he heard about it he came tearing over to our student house in his car, brakes screeching as he parked up outside. He charged into the house with a bag full of defence devices for our protection: there were dozens of rape alarms and pepper sprays that would not only sting an assailant's eyes, but also dye his face blue so that he could be easily identified in a line-up.

For me he had something special – a flick knife. I told him that if I carried a blade I'd be committing a criminal offence, but he brushed aside my concerns. If I were attacked, he said, I should 'stab the fucker'.

Before I could raise any more objections, Dad had marched back out to his car and sped away with a deafening 'Vrrrooooom'. I have no idea where he got the self-defence kit from.

Dad loved to give Mum clothes and jewellery. He didn't buy her flashy baubles; instead he bought her delicate diamonds and subtle pearls. He would regularly comment on how chic and elegant she was. He'd say, 'Your mother can walk into a room in a simple dress and knock the spots off every other woman there.' Mum would disagree with this, but it's what he often said.

When my brother was born, Dad went to Penhaligon's and asked for one of everything in the shop.

When it came to money, my parents balanced each other out. Where he was impetuous, she was practical. Dad earned the money, and Mum managed it. While Dad liked the things that money could buy, he wasn't especially materialistic. It was a means to an end. Dad didn't only educate his own children with the money he earned, he also contributed to Natalie and Simon's, my mum's sister's kids' school fees, as well as looking after Granddad in his old age.

Dad faced criticism for some of the films he was in. He took certain jobs for the money and didn't always make the shrewdest career decisions. Some people accused him of selling out but, as ever, he didn't give a damn. Providing for us was his priority.

As he aged, he took a more relaxed attitude to his job. 'The cameo [role] is the governor,' he used to say. 'You go in there for a couple of weeks, you're paid a lot of money, everybody treats you like the Crown jewels, you're in and out and, if the film's a load of shit, nobody blames you.'

I remember when I was eleven years old, one weekday morning, I knew he was leaving to go on a job. It was five o'clock and the sound of him plodding down the stairs woke me. By the time I was out of bed it was too late to say goodbye – he was out the door.

I scurried to my bedroom window, which faced on to the street. I watched him wheel his case over to the waiting car. The driver took his bags and put them in the boot. Dad didn't get into the car straight away. He leaned against the passenger door and looked up at our house. I peeked through the blinds – for some reason I didn't want him to see me. He stared for several minutes, looking wistful but resigned. After some time spent gazing at our house, he got in the car and was driven away. I never told him that I saw him looking up. It had felt as though I was intruding on a private moment.

Dad loved his work, but he kept it in perspective. He missed us when he went away, and as soon as he came home he would shut the door on the world.

CHAPTER TEN

I SPENT MUCH OF my childhood waiting for Dad to come home. He'd wheel his case into the kitchen and flop down on a chair, relieved to be back.

I still find myself expecting him to walk through the door, saying, 'Make us a cup of tea please, love.'

I didn't know it at the time, but those ordinary moments, when he was well, were the good old days.

Grief ebbs and flows like the tide. Often it's a quiet hum in the background, like persistent tinnitus. At other times it can be overwhelming and unbearable. No matter what stage in the tidal cycle, it's constant.

The void that Dad has left behind is merciless and bleak. He was unique, irreplaceable. I kid myself into thinking that one day I'll wake up to the realisation that it's all a dream, and he was never ill at all.

Today isn't special: I'm just sitting at the kitchen table trying to write, in the chair that he liked to sit in, listening to the ticking of the railway clock that used to hang in our kitchen in Sussex. I'm glad that my kitten, Cleo, is here. Her presence breaks the isolation. She has hopped on to the table and placed her little paws on my left wrist while I type. It limits my movement somewhat, but her purr is comforting.

I never thought it was possible to miss someone this much. Previously I'd assumed that yearning is finite – there can only be so much room in one heart for any one person – but I was wrong. The longing. The desperation for just one more conversation. The feeble, deluded hope that I will call my parents' house and he'll pick up and say, "Ello, love.'

My mum's home number is still listed as 'Mum and Dad' on my mobile. I see no reason to rename my contacts list. I decide to take a break and visit Mum. I can't bear to leave Cleo so I bundle her into her travel box and we head off. I let Cleo out when we get to Mum's and she sets about exploring every nook and cranny of this new place. While Mum puts the kettle on, I go upstairs to the room where she stores Dad's things. I run my fingers over his silk ties, put my hands in the pockets of his coats.

He only wore one cologne: Monsieur Balmain. There's still a bottle of it in the bathroom cabinet. I lift it to my nose and breathe in the scent deeply. It smells clean, of lemons and sandalwood. I spray some on my wrist.

Mum calls from downstairs. The tea is getting cold and

Cleo has got into her pots and pans cupboard. I pad down, extract the squirming kitten from a colander and take my place at the kitchen table. While we drink the tea, we talk about how much we miss him and how it actually hurts physically. There's a constant dull ache in my chest and a tightness in my throat. We talk about how close it all feels, as though he died yesterday, and then suddenly how it all seems so far away, as if it happened to somebody else.

Cleo seems to have tired herself out so I take her home. On the way back – as I so often do – I find myself remembering Dad's last days.

In the final forty-eight hours in hospital, Dad's eyes grew dull. He was absent. But in the days before the lights went out, he had looked at me with untainted affection. He was almost paralysed and unable to look away but, even if he could, I don't think he'd wanted to. His eyes had shone above the oxygen mask, the tubes, wires and beeping machines.

I let myself back in and hurry to my laptop. I want to write this recollection down before I forget it. I find myself sobbing. I type the words just quick enough before the tears take over and I have to stop. However much I try to carry on writing, I can't. The screen swims before me and once again I'm swept under by a wave of grief.

• • •

People seldom speak ill of the dead. It's as if departure from this world excludes them from any criticism or honest reflection. It would be easy to fall into the trap of idolising Dad, like I did when I was a young girl. Remembering him as he was keeps his memory closer to me – the real man stays nearby.

My dad wasn't always an easy man to be close to. When I was a little girl I craved his attention more than anything. As I grew older, he was often emotionally unavailable and distant. I cherished any time I got to spend with him and did my utmost to be the perfect daughter, always happy, clever, talented and undemanding. But whatever I did, it didn't seem to make any difference. Dad's instinct was to lock himself away and hermetically seal himself from the world.

When I was a teenager we lived in a house in Belsize Park, north London. Dad designed a man cave on the ground floor. It was a spacious, oak-panelled room filled with dark leather furniture. The walls were covered with exotic artefacts that he had carried home from his travels. Attached to his study was a small darkroom that he used for developing his photographs.

After his death, I come across a photo of me that he took at Christmas when I was in my early twenties. I've forgotten all about it. He printed the photo in black and white, colour and sepia and experimented with tone. All in all there are a dozen copies of this one photo. He kept them in a folder full of every handmade birthday card I had given him as a child. He was gentle and occasionally prone to sentimentality. But for a lot of the time he kept that side of himself hidden away.

Dad's man cave was peppered with cameras and lenses. The shelves were bursting with books: classic novels, gothic dramas, plays, science fiction, archaeological texts and tomes on ancient mathematics. Despite his scant education he was well read and interested in many subjects. His music collection was vast and eclectic, ranging from Shostakovich to John Lee Hooker, the Rolling Stones, Joe Cocker, Billie Holiday, Bob Dylan, Miles Davis and Mozart. His taste was broad yet discerning.

Once he'd finished a job, Dad would distance himself from the experience of it and hide away in his man cave. He described this process as 'flushing'. At the time I could be hurt by this detachment, but with the benefit of hindsight it's clear he needed that quiet time in order to do his job. However, the 'flushing' didn't always work.

In 1998 he made a film called *Felicia's Journey*. Directed by Atom Egoyan, and based on William Trevor's prize-winning novel of the same name, *Felicia's Journey* is a psychological thriller which tells the story of Felicia (Elaine Cassidy), an Irish teenager who travels to England hoping to find the boy-friend who has made her pregnant. While she is there, she accepts the help of a middle-aged catering manager called

Joseph Hilditch (played by Dad), who appears friendly but has a secret and sinister backstory.

Two weeks after he'd returned home from filming, Mum told Dad that he was behaving very strangely. For a man who didn't believe in Method acting, he seemed to be having trouble leaving Hilditch behind.

Dad liked his own little world. He loved listening to stories, and would often potter around the kitchen or his darkroom, plugged into his headphones. Or he'd hunker down in his study and shut himself away from the world. At root he was a private, solitary man.

He kept a secret stash of whisky in leather-bound bottles on a shelf above his desk. To my knowledge he didn't get drunk on a regular basis on his own in the man cave, but I'm pretty sure he would have the occasional tipple of an evening. There was one occasion when I walked in to find him drunk off his arse. I never ratted him out to my mother; I just rolled my eyes and left him to it.

Dad wasn't an alcoholic by any means, but his relationship with alcohol wasn't always healthy. Since his death, his old friends and colleagues have all spoken about his drinking habits. Before he met my mother he was wild and sometimes out of control. Afterwards, he calmed down. His hellraising tendencies mellowed but never totally disappeared.

Despite his occasional emotional distance, I felt a powerful bond with my dad that was mostly unspoken. My relationship with my mother is and always has been one of constant chatter – we can talk for hours. Dad and I were more similar, but fewer words were exchanged. We shared many of the same character traits: quick to anger but also quick to laughter, generosity, unreasonable impatience, impulsivity and a garrulous streak that can sometimes lead to drinking too much and telling rude jokes, often at the wrong time and in the wrong place.

Looking back now, it's odd that I never became more accustomed to Dad's transient presence in my life. It happened often enough – I should have grown inured to it. When he was away I felt a duty to be as well behaved as I could in order to lighten the load. No one ever said that it was up to me to do this, and Mum held everything together without a problem. But I felt I carried the responsibility anyway.

On an unconscious level, I think Dad passed on the duty baton that his father had given to him. Although neither of my parents abdicated responsibility in the way Granddad did, I nevertheless internalised the pattern. He had been lumbered with more than his young shoulders could bear. It's funny how family dysfunction seeps down through the generations, even when everyone makes a concerted effort to break the pattern.

On one occasion, when I was sixteen and Dad and I were on a long car journey in Sussex, heading to a garden centre,

I opened up to him about the anxiety I experienced whenever he was away, and how I felt it was my job to look after everyone. He was saddened and dismayed because he recognised the pattern and was desperate to avoid the mistakes his parents had made. We talked about it. He told me that it was not my job to be a stand-in caretaker when he was gone. But my core belief was set. I tried to make myself as unneedy as possible, and I kept a lot of things secret from the family. Mum often says that when I was a teenager I was well behaved at home but loud and challenging at school. There were periods when I was picked on by other kids or was having a rough time with teachers, but I rarely told my parents.

Whenever Dad came back, I could breathe a sigh of relief as I felt the weight being lifted from my shoulders. Logically, I knew that my mother and brother were fine and they didn't need me to take responsibility for their welfare. But I couldn't shake the feeling that if I slacked off the family would fall apart. I tried to make myself seem as capable and together as possible. This was a recipe for disaster. It's impossible to control the well-being of one's loved ones – we are only ever really in charge of ourselves.

As a teenager I struggled with all the normal insecurities and hang-ups synonymous with the hellish transition from childhood to adulthood. From the age of twelve I suffered from trichotillomania, an impulse-control disorder that results in the urge to pull out one's own hair. I tried to hide my behaviour from my parents for as long as possible; I didn't want to worry them. I talked to Mum about little parts of it, but I didn't feel that I could reveal the full extent of my destructive habits. When they did notice that I had pulled out chunks of hair from my head and picked away at my eyelashes, naturally they were concerned and upset.

Dad especially found my trichotillomania very difficult to deal with. He hated the idea that his little girl was disfiguring herself. When I was fourteen, I pulled out all of my eyelashes and was so horrified and ashamed of myself that I shut myself away in my room. There was a knock at the door. Dad came in and sat on the bed where I was lying, facing away from him.

He put his hand on my head and said, 'It's all right, love. I remember this feeling: you feel that everything about you is wrong. It's not true. It'll be all right. Your lashes will grow back and you'll be fine.'

'How do you know?' I asked.

'I just know,' he said.

His reassurance meant a lot to me and he was right, the eyelashes grew back. But I needed a lot more help in order to be 'fine'.

My parents did as much as they could to support me and sent me to various specialists. I saw hypnotherapists, counsellors and doctors to try to stop me self-harming. The hair-pulling became worse at times of stress. During my exams, I would wake up with hair wound around my fingers after I had yanked it out in my sleep.

Self-harm is a vicious cycle that feeds upon itself. The more one self-harms, the more shame and embarrassment one feels. This, in turn, causes stress and increases the tendency to self-harm. Throughout most of my teenage years I wore thick black kohl and false lashes to cover up my bald eyelids. I had a good go at the hair on my head too, but it was never as notice-able as the loss of my eyelashes.

One of the practitioners I saw was an art therapist. I had sessions with her in my early twenties. She was a calming presence and in her cosy room I was able to work through some of my issues. We would talk for a while and then she would encourage me to draw. It didn't matter whether the drawing was good or not – it was just an expression of feel-ings. It was helpful to get everything out of my head and on to the page, like a kind of visual exorcism.

One day the art therapist suggested that I should ask Dad to come to a session with me, so I could tell him all the things I felt unable to say under normal circumstances. She could see that I craved closeness with him; that I needed to hear his words and, in turn, be heard by him.

To Dad's credit, he was happy to come with me, and he

drove us to the clinic in Marylebone on a sunny November morning. We both sat down in the therapist's comfortable chairs but I couldn't talk. Not a sound. He was right there, waiting to hear what I had to say, but the words wouldn't come. My throat closed up and I stuttered and fidgeted.

The discomfort in the room became too much for him and he stood up, muttering something about having to go and check the parking meter. A few minutes later he came back and we started again. I was desperate to articulate my feelings but, yet again, I couldn't find my voice. This time he started to fidget and squirm and off he went again, downstairs and out of the building to check on his car. When he was gone, the therapist asked me if Dad's behaviour was making me angry. Yes, I said. It was making me furious.

By the time he got back I was burning with rage. The art therapist gave him a sound telling-off. I had never heard anyone chastise him in that way before and get away with it. He bowed his head and nodded: he knew he was being evasive. Suddenly, the fury burst out of me in a stream of tears. Words that I had held in for years poured out. I told him that I needed him, that I missed him when he was gone, that I felt an unwieldy responsibility and that I was worried that one day I would lose my mind completely.

Dad listened, looking sad and crestfallen. I think he would have done anything to take it all away. He said he was sorry, that he would keep the door to the man cave open, that he would do his best to make himself available to me.

By the end of the appointment we both felt raw and vulnerable. We walked out into the biting winter air in silence and got in the car. Instead of driving home to Belsize Park, he took a detour to St John's Wood. We parked up on the High Street – he didn't tell me where we were going. He led me into a jeweller's shop and told me to pick out whatever I wanted.

I told him I didn't want him to buy me anything, but he insisted. His attention was drawn to a chunky silver necklace that looked like a spiny row of teeth. It was heavy and beautifully made. The assistant lifted it out of the glass case and helped me try it on. It sat snugly on my collar bones and framed my throat. There was something reassuring about its weight, as if it were a suit of armour for the place where my words got stuck.

Was Dad trying to buy his way out of emotional intimacy? At the time I thought he might be, but now I realise he was using the only vocabulary available to him to tell me he loved me. I still have the spiny necklace to this day. I wear it whenever I need strength.

CHAPTER ELEVEN

I SUPPOSE IT WAS only natural that I should have wanted to follow my dad into acting. I think artistic and creative tendencies might be genetic and it was no surprise to my parents when I expressed a desire to be an actress. I was in lots of plays at school and loved it. Because of my dyslexia, I'd found a lot of lessons frustrating. There was a disparity between what I was capable of putting on the page, and what was going on in my head. For many years I was convinced I was stupid, and I never believed I could do something as academic as write a book. But whenever I was on stage everything seemed to make sense. The fact that I regularly came last in maths and science exams was suddenly irrelevant.

For as long as I can remember I've felt like an outsider. I do a passable job of blending in most of the time, but the sense that I don't belong is constantly rattling around in the back of my mind. I was terrible at being 'cool': I was boisterous and enthusiastic, far too lively to ever fit into the cool crowd. Not that I minded too much – the 'in crowd' at my school were as dull as ditchwater.

But when I was in a theatre, my loud personality was no longer a problem. I did work experience at the National Theatre in the summer of 1999, when I was sixteen. Trevor Nunn was directing a season. Although I was shy and awkward at first, I did feel at home. That being said, on the first day of my placement I managed to spill a cup of coffee down my front. I was mortified but no one seemed to notice. There was a vase of flowers on the tea and coffee table: I bent over the flowers to hide my spillage while I figured out what to do. One of the actors spotted me stranded behind the flowers. He sent me to wardrobe, where the wardrobe mistress very sweetly washed my top and gave me a shirt to wear. I went back to the rehearsal room in a man's ruffled shirt, which looked like it belonged in an eighteenth-century costume drama. Despite my mishap, the people there made me feel very at home.

At the time there was a rep company performing a few plays simultaneously. The company would rehearse one play during the day, and they'd perform another in the evening. I observed the show from the audience, backstage and during rehearsal. I'd spent a lot of time on film sets, but this was my first experience of professional theatre. I loved it. At the time I thought that this world would give me a place to belong.

By the time my A levels came around, I was sure I wanted to be an actress. However, the teachers at my school recommended that I study drama at university, rather than go to drama school. It seemed more sensible to have a qualification that could be used elsewhere, in case acting didn't pan out. Also, Dad didn't have many good things to say about traditionally trained actors. He maintained that whenever he worked with a young actor fresh out of drama school, they would have to go through a period of unlearning their training before they could actually get on with the job.

I went to Middlesex University, where I met my future husband and a circle of friends, most of whom I'm still very close with. I enjoyed the course, but sometimes I was frustrated that it wasn't more focused on acting. In a way, drama school might have been a better choice for me after all. But then I wouldn't have met Peter, so I've no regrets about going to Middlesex.

I left university in 2005 with an absurd goal: I thought I should be a film star within the year. People say that to really succeed in acting, you have to want it so much that you'll die if you don't get it. That was certainly true of me. In retrospect, I think I wanted it too much. Having worked in professional theatre, both on stage and backstage, I now realise the sense of belonging I had found at the National Theatre was temporary. For years I was convinced there was no other place for me – my whole identity was tied up in being an actress.

Much to my naive surprise, my plan didn't work out. I would often get down to the last two in auditions, but I had trouble landing the job. I was too tall, too pretty, not pretty enough, too posh, not posh enough, or just plain 'not right for the role'. Sometimes I wonder if being my dad's daughter worked against me. I think casting directors used to expect a female version of him, and were thrown when they discovered how different I was.

Whatever the reason, it was frustrating and disappointing, mostly because I usually had great feedback from the auditions. When casting directors would call my agent, they had positive things to say about me – just not the good news of my having landed the part. I have no idea whether they were being honest or not, but it used to make me glad and deflated in equal measure.

When I first started acting, I would go to see Dad every time I had an audition. We would read the lines together and he would give me suggestions about my performance. He had absolute confidence that I would get the part. Whenever I expressed doubt that my acting career wouldn't work out, he'd furrow his brow and look as though I had suggested that pigs had just flown past the window. 'Don't be daft!' he'd say. 'Of course you're going to make it.'

Whenever I failed to land a part, he'd be shocked. 'What do you mean they didn't give it to you? Well, fuck 'em then.

They obviously wouldn't know talent if it smacked them in the face.'

Reading lines with Dad was interesting. He wasn't great at cold reading: it was the one part of being an actor that he struggled with.

When he'd first read a script with me, he would fumble the words. The only thing, acting-wise, that Dad could never have done is narrate audiobooks.

Despite his sometimes clumsy readings, he gave great directions. The first job I ever landed was a guest role in *Midsomer Murders*. I played a rather glum girl whose mother has been murdered in the kitchen with a saucepan. I had a big courtroom scene where my character has to testify against the prime suspect in her mother's murder and break down under the pressure.

Before the casting I prepared a dramatic interpretation of the script, complete with weeping and wailing.

Dad suggested I dispense with the histrionics and focus on trying to hold in the pain. He said, 'It's always more moving watching someone who is fighting to hold it together.'

I read the lines again, this time as he had suggested.

'Do it like that and you'll get the part,' he said.

And I did.

It didn't always work, mind you. There were several times when I followed his advice and was disappointed. After the first year it dawned on me that it wasn't going to be as easy for me as it had been for Dad. I didn't have the knack of being totally in the moment and committed to the role, but then able to shrug it off as though it didn't matter. It meant too much to me; being successful was tangled up with earning my dad's praise and approval.

After he had watched a performance of mine, either on TV or on stage, a proud grin would spread across Dad's face and he would open his arms for a big hug. For a moment, my anxiety would be muzzled and everything would seem all right. Looking back, I can see why I wasn't getting the work: I took all of my baggage into auditions with me. Even though I was giving consistently solid performances, I was holding a part of myself back. Now when I go into castings I'm more relaxed. I am no longer fretting about the job or trying to impress my dad. I have other projects to focus on, and losing him has put it all into context.

But back in my mid-twenties I was ashamed that I wasn't as successful as Dad. I don't think he was ever out of work a day in his whole life. If he wasn't working, it was because he didn't want to. I was desperate to be as good as him and achieve what he had achieved. It was a fool's game – one he never asked me to play. He honestly didn't care whether I was successful or not. He just wanted me to be happy.

Nothing could reassure me, though. I felt as if his success

drew my failure into sharp contrast. I felt awkward and mediocre in his shadow. I became convinced that I was a dull-witted loser and an embarrassment to my family. I barely left the flat I shared with Peter, except to go to the off-licence and pick up some drink. Quitting acting seemed inevitable. The idea of giving up on my dreams led me to despair, but the thought of carrying on and exposing my battered ego to more rejection was also unbearable. It seemed that whatever choice I made would result in further disappointment and failure.

Eventually, Peter suggested to me that I go on a residential therapy course called the Hoffman Process. I didn't want to but, at the time, it seemed to be my only option.

The process worked for me. What I learned there was profound and moving. I gained insight into my flawed coping mechanisms and came back stronger and healthier. Looking back on it now, my misery seems ridiculous and self-indulgent, but at the time I couldn't see it for what it was.

The day after I came home from the Hoffman Process I went over to my parents' house. They were both anxious to see me. I had been in such a terrible state when I'd left that they must have worried about me while I was away. (Any contact with the outside world is forbidden during the process.)

We sat down and had a cup of tea and Dad slipped into his default mode of trying to distract me with some of his funnier anecdotes. As I had grown older, this had become one of the things about him that made me furious. He was always telling a joke or trying to mask what was really going on by distracting everyone's attention. It was his coping mechanism, but it drove me crazy. What I had learned at Hoffman emboldened me to confront him.

'Dad,' I said, 'stop acting. You don't need to do that with me.'

I'd never seen him look so nonplussed. 'I don't?' he said.

'No, you don't. You don't have to entertain me. Just be my dad – that's all I need from you.'

'Oh. Right then.'

After that day, something shifted. We slowly bridged a gap between us. From that point onwards, our relationship became more comfortable and honest. The unspoken tension evaporated and we became easy and calm in each other's company. It was as if someone had thrown open the windows in a stuffy room and let in a spring breeze to clear out the old cobwebs.

CHAPTER TWELVE

THE MAN I MARRIED ten days after my twenty-seventh birthday is nothing like my father, and nothing like me. Having two explosive, impulsive personalities in one relationship would be bedlam.

Peter is calm, sensible and easy-going and we balance each other well. We've been together since I was nineteen and he was twenty-one. We were in a student production of *Under Milk Wood* at Middlesex. According to him, he had a crush on me from the start but was too shy to make a move. I didn't fancy him at first, but after getting to know him a bit I developed quite a crush on him too. We got together and within a couple of weeks I knew that Peter was the man I was going to marry.

When he first met Dad, Peter was anxious. We'd arranged a meeting over dinner in Lemonia, a Greek restaurant in Primrose Hill that my family often went to. We arrived early and I tried to reassure Pete that it would be fine: Dad wasn't actually Harold Shand, and if he failed to make a good impression, he would not find himself strung by his feet in an abattoir.

When my parents and Jack appeared, Dad sat opposite

Peter. He was outwardly polite, shook Pete's hand and said, 'Nice to meet you,' but I could tell Dad was eyeing this new boyfriend with suspicion.

Not that I blamed him. I'd been out with a spectacular selection of dullards in the past. My parents hadn't disliked every boy I'd brought home out of principle – there had been one or two they'd been fond of. But most of them were not met with approval because they were, at best, unsuitable and, at worst, downright idiots. Fortunately they had the presence of mind to keep their disapproval to themselves, knowing full well that the more they disliked any lad, the more I was likely to run into his arms. When the romance inevitably would end in tears, they'd provide tea and sympathy whilst privately punching the air with glee.

Dad wasn't quite as adept as my mother at hiding his joy when a doomed relationship finally bit the dust. After I'd dumped one particularly dim-witted boy, he said, 'You're better off without that one, love. He was a right mumphead.'

Although I was heartbroken and convinced I would never love again, he had a valid point.

Dad's suspicion that Pete was another idiot took a while to calm. His paternal protectiveness was usually held off at an appropriate distance. He didn't interfere in my business as a matter of course. However, when aggravated he could be fearsome.

When I was eighteen I'd gone to visit him in Rome, where

he was playing the Pope in a TV drama (imaginatively called *The Good Pope: Pope John XXIII*). This was the first and only time I visited him alone. On his day off, we had been strolling through the city on our way to the Colosseum when Dad got sidetracked by the tantalising sight of a butcher's window. (He was a committed carnivore – another trait I inherited.)

Oblivious to his detour, I'd ambled on down the street without him. In the twenty seconds or so that we were separated, a slimy-looking man sauntered over and started to purr Italian in my ear. I'd looked around and realised I couldn't see Dad. Then I'd heard a ferocious bark behind my back and a beefy hand grabbed my arm. Dad yanked me away and, in that moment, I had seen the raw aggression that Dad attributed to being 'from the street'. The man backed off quickly as Dad hustled me down the road.

'Fucking liberty,' he'd grumbled.

We never spoke of it again.

The first dinner with Pete and my family at Lemonia went smoothly. When he got to know him well enough to see that he wasn't an idiot, Dad was delighted that I had chosen a partner who was the polar opposite to him. They got on well to begin with, and then bonded properly after dinner one summer's evening. Mum and I were getting on with clearing the dishes inside and Dad and Peter sat in the garden, drinking wine and eating cheese.

In my dad's final months, I think it was a comfort for him to know that he was leaving me happily married to a good man.

After we'd been together for seven years, Pete proposed to me at home on Valentine's Day. I was delighted and slightly shocked. I called my parents, who were thrilled.

Pete later apologised to Dad for not asking for his permission.

'Don't worry, mate,' said Dad, 'help yourself!'

After much planning and organising, the day of the wedding came around. My eyes snapped open at six o'clock in the morning. I had had a fitful and excited night's sleep. I padded downstairs to the sunlit kitchen to find my dad in his navy-blue dressing gown.

'Hello, love,' he said, 'you're up early. Tea?'

'Yes, please,' I said.

Dad bustled off to put the kettle on and fished out a mug emblazoned with the letter R from the crockery cupboard. He returned with a steaming mug of hot tea.

'Sleep well?' he asked.

'Not especially. I was too nervous and excited.'

'Yeah. Me too.'

He was doing his best to hide it from me but I could tell that Dad was racked with anxiety. I had never noticed him being jittery about anything before. After some questioning, I managed to prise it out of him: 'I don't want to let you down.'

I was stunned. How could the most confident man I'd ever known be nervous about walking me down the aisle and giving a speech? His performances had been watched by millions of people all over the world. Surely speaking in front of 120 people was going to be easy? We expected an emotional day, but Dad's anxiety was out of place.

'Don't worry, Dad,' I said. 'You'll be fine. And you won't let me down. You never could.'

In retrospect, I think I was too wrapped up in my own nerves to engage with his anxiety. We sat together in silent apprehension, sipping tea. Dad having stage fright was a new experience for me and I couldn't think of anything to say. So I scurried upstairs to take a bath and start getting ready.

At nine o'clock, Alan the hairdresser and my trio of bridesmaids – Carolyn, Alex and Alice, my three best friends from university – arrived. In an instant the house was full of excited chatter and tinkling laughter; the girls and I had known each other for years and shared the familiarity of sisters.

After my hair was teased into rollers, I went upstairs to start on my make-up. Women always look ridiculous in rollers. I went into my parents' bathroom, which has two sinks. I ensconced myself at Mum's mirror and slowly applied careful layers of make-up. I was vaguely aware of Dad at his sink, having a shave and performing the male equivalent of the slow, considered ritual that I was absorbed in. I continued applying subtle make-up until I was satisfied. I turned and asked Dad what he thought.

One of Dad's lesser-known traits was that he was good at giving fashion and make-up advice. There were several occasions when I lived at home when he'd do a double take, frown at some aspect of my appearance and tell me that my shade of lipstick didn't suit me, that my coat was the wrong shape or my hair was getting too long. Once, when I was wearing a backless evening dress during the day, he turned to me and said, 'That's a nice dress you're almost wearing, love.'

His critique was often unwelcome, especially if it came when I was just about to go out. I'd regularly flout his suggestion and assert my independence and individualism. He was invariably right, though, which was irritating in the extreme but ultimately useful. As the years passed, I grew out of my tendency to disregard his suggestions just for the sake of it. His advice wasn't intended to repress my individuality: he liked that I was rather eccentric and flamboyant. However, if I wore something that made me look like a prat – a ridiculous hat, say, or lurid pink tights – he would tell me in no uncertain terms.

On my wedding day, he studied my face closely and told me that I looked 'startlingly beautiful', despite the rollers. Of course he was biased, but it meant the world to me. And I knew that if my make-up wasn't right I could have depended on him to tell me.

Alan the hairdresser unwound my hair and swept it up into a soft bun. With the help of Mum and my bridesmaids, I slipped into my wedding dress – a silk gown with jewelled embellishments over the shoulders. My bridesmaids wore matching strapless cream dresses with silver beading across the bodices. Alan placed dainty white flowers in their hair.

While I dressed, the house filled up with people. Tori, our little flower girl, arrived with her mum Denise. Tori wore a white and silver floaty dress with a garland of white flowers in her hair. My older half-brother Alex, my younger brother Jack, the bridesmaids and flower girl, Alan, assorted friends of the family and the photographer were milling around the kitchen. When I came downstairs, the photographer started snapping. One of my most prized possessions is the image of Dad and I together, standing in the garden. We look happy and excited.

The time came for us to leave and make our way to London Zoo, where the wedding was to take place. We chose the zoo because it was a central London location that had the capacity to fit all the guests. Most importantly, it wasn't ostentatious. We'd thought about Claridge's, the Savoy or the Dorchester, but they all seemed too grandiose. Even though Dad earned good money, he wasn't flashy, and a fancy hotel didn't feel appropriate for our family. Plus, London Zoo was where Mum and Dad had gone on their first date.

Mum and the bridesmaids piled into one car and Dad and I were driven to the zoo in a vintage Bentley. There are certain curious traditions around births, weddings and funerals and the car journey for the bride and her father is one of those bizarre rites of passage. If you step back and analyse these traditions they're rather archaic, although the time we had together was a moment of fundamental importance for both Dad and me.

It was a hot and humid June day and the air inside the car was stifling. When I'd picked the car, I hadn't factored in a heatwave or the car's lack of air conditioning. We wound down the windows but the air was so still that it didn't help. The car was festooned with bridal ribbons and was attracting a lot of attention on the streets of north London. People not only stopped and stared, they smiled and waved. We even got applause from a minivan full of brightly dressed African women. I think they must have been off to a wedding themselves.

Dad was nervous in the car. He knew that custom dictated he should give his daughter some sage words of advice at this point, but he was stumped. He looked out of the window and fidgeted.

As we made our way towards Regent's Park, we cruised down Kentish Town Road, creeping along in the congested

Saturday-afternoon traffic. The Bentley caught the eye of a man on the pavement to our right. He looked at the car, looked at me, looked at Dad, recognised him, did a double take, and walked slap bang into a lamp post.

Dad and I burst into helpless hysterics. The poor fellow might have broken his nose for all we knew, but the traffic lights changed and we drove on before we could see if his face was gushing with blood or not. The spontaneous laughter broke the tension in the car at last and Dad relaxed.

He found his words. 'Listen, love,' he said. 'I'm not going to tell you how to have a happy marriage because you're already happy with Pete, so there's nothing more that I can say. Just don't rush having kids, even though I'd love it. Take your time.'

There are some parts of my wedding day that I can't remember because I was too excited, but those moments with Dad in the car are seared into my memory.

The ceremony was due to take place at 5 p.m. but Dad and I arrived with almost an hour to spare, so the driver took us around the park until the time came to pull into the back entrance of London Zoo. Mum and I had spent months planning every detail of the wedding, so the event flowed without a hitch.

The venue was an art deco, crescent-shaped building facing

Regent's Park on one side and emus and wallabies on the other. As we arrived, the last of the guests were peering at the animals before going in to take their seats. The bridesmaids had congregated at the Komodo dragon house, which was the designated spot for meeting the registrar. It was one of the more surreal experiences of my life, spelling out my and my husband's names as a hefty Komodo dragon lumbered past with its tongue curiously licking the air. My heart was in my mouth and my chief bridesmaid placed her hand on my chest to feel the thump-thumping in my ribcage.

Once the registrar was satisfied, we made our way to the open doors of the ceremony venue. I slipped my arm into Dad's and we simultaneously took a deep breath. The string quartet played the opening chords of 'Moon River' and Tori toddled ahead of us with her woven basket of rose petals, chucking them on the floor with hilarious disdain, as though they were nasty, sticky things to be discarded. After the first four bars of music, Dad and I stepped into the doorway and slowly made our way down the aisle. I suddenly felt overwhelmed. It hadn't really occurred to me that a room crowded with people would turn to look at me. Dad's thick arm proved a sturdy and much-needed support. The faces of my family and friends swam before my eyes, until Pete suddenly came into focus. He was beaming.

I was on the edge of bursting into tears when I turned to Dad. He looked prouder than I had ever seen him. In heels I was a good six inches taller than him, and I had to bend down to hug him. He grasped me in his arms for a long moment, slightly rocking me to and fro. He let me go, then took my bouquet and sat down next to Mum in the front row.

During the ceremony Peter and I shared vows that we had written ourselves. When the registrar asked if there were any legal impediments to our union, only an emu screeched his disapproval.

An opera friend of ours sang 'O mio babbino caro' from the Puccini opera *Gianni Schicchi.* Lyrically, it's an inappropriate choice for a wedding: it tells the story of a young woman begging her father to let her marry the boy she loves, because if she doesn't get her way she'll throw herself in the river. In hindsight, the aria is perfect – the title translated into English is 'Oh my Beloved Father'.

Directly after we were married, Peter and I wandered around the zoo with the wedding photographer and had our picture taken standing in front of the animals in their enclosures. A grouchy tigress stalked forward and snarled her disapproval. (Maybe she knew that the punters had all gone home and she was not impressed to be working overtime.) Some of my favourite pictures from the day are of Pete and I smiling, blissfully unaware of the sour-faced tiger scowling behind us.

• • •

Our wedding flew by, and I struggle to pick out particular moments.

To remind myself, I pore over the hundreds of photographs we have and watch our wedding video. When I originally watched the footage, I only had eyes for Pete. Now when I watch it, all I see is Dad.

When he gave his speech, Dad spoke with all his usual charisma and charm. He looked delighted, and he wasn't acting. I didn't notice it at the time, but he was starting to show early signs of his disease. His nerves were only a small part of the growing anxiety that was gnawing away at his confidence.

It was one of the happiest days of all our lives. We seem so innocent, wrapped up in the moment, oblivious to the looming tragedy about to crash down upon us. Within sixteen months of the wedding, Dad would be diagnosed with the illness which was to rob us of him for ever.

CHAPTER THIRTEEN

WHEN DAD WAS ALIVE, I tended not to watch his performances unless we went to a premiere or the opening night of a play. There were occasions, of course, when he was proud of a performance and would ask me to watch it with him. When he was in an episode of *The Street* in 2009 – the one for which he went on to win an international Emmy – he sat me down and asked for my opinion. He played Paddy, a reformed-alcoholic pub landlord whose livelihood – and life – are endangered when he takes a principled stand in banning the son of a local thug for smoking in the pub toilets. I thought his performance was wonderful and I told him so. Of course I'm biased in his favour, but since he did win the Emmy for the role, I wasn't too far off.

In a way, Dad lives on through his work. I can always visit him at the push of a button. When most people die, they only exist in the recollections of those people who knew them. The deceased may leave possessions, a few photos, maybe a home movie or two. But mostly when people die they float away into oblivion. My generation records every second of their lives. Perhaps it's a desire to become immortal – the ghosts of our holidays, weddings and Sunday lunches will haunt social media long after we're all gone.

As the fog of illness slowly descended over Dad's faculties, it would have been unbearable to watch him performing at the pinnacle of his powers. But now that he is gone, I find myself drawn back towards the DVD cupboard. I want to watch some of his work as part of the research process.

I can access Dad from his thirties to his sixties. I feel lucky to have him at my fingertips. I'll never forget what he looked like, or the sound of his laugh. Perhaps, in years to come, this will be a comfort, but, at present, forcing myself to sit through his career, film after film, is an ordeal. I develop a pattern: I procrastinate for a few days, then I force myself to turn on the TV and ram in the DVD. About fifteen minutes into a film I start to forget that he's dead and I become engrossed in the story. But when the credits roll, the bleak reality that he's gone for good will come crashing down on me again.

Some performances affect me more than others. In *The Street*, for example, he is very close to the Dad who walked me down the aisle. His walk is a little slower, his posture slightly more hunched than in his previous incarnations. This is the Dad I lost.

However, the reality dawns on me that this isn't really him. It's a recording of an actor doing his job. I'm left in emotional and mental limbo – it's hard to truly accept that he's dead while he's alive and well on the TV. I wish I believed in heaven.

How comforting it must be for people of faith to believe their loved ones are safely tucked away in a better place.

I find the dusty box set of *Pennies from Heaven*, long forgotten at the back of the cupboard, wedged beside *Mona Lisa*. I realise it will be essential viewing. It sits on the kitchen table for a number of weeks, still in its wrapper. Eventually, I tear off the cellophane and shove the DVD in the machine without ceremony. A 35-year-old Dad springs to life on the screen. I am prepared to be swept under by a tidal wave of grief but for once the tears stay away. I soon forget that I am watching Dad and become lost in the story.

This incarnation of Dad – whose black hair hasn't yet receded and gone white and whose face is unlined – this Dad doesn't upset me, because he is so removed from the father I am grieving every day. However, as I watch him live out Arthur Parker's surreal tragedy, I catch sight of my younger brother's expressions flitting across his face. They have the same hazel eyes and dark, thick eyelashes. The smile, the laugh – there's so much of Jack there. It's reassuring to know that Dad's spirit lives on in Jack.

I find comfort watching him in his prime. It reminds me that he wasn't always ill – that he was once electric, full of crackling talent and energy.

I watch the entire series in one sitting. It draws to a close, and Arthur is sentenced to death. The song 'Pennies from

Heaven', sung by Arthur Tracy, rings out, and a beam of light is projected on to Dad. Having remained intact up until this point, I suddenly break. Bitter tears spring from nowhere. I wish, more than anything, that I believed in heaven.

In the run-up to Dad's diagnosis in 2011, I'd noticed that something seemed wrong, but had pushed the thought into the farthest recesses of my mind. On reflection, the signs were clear. His unshakeable confidence diminished and he became nervous about things that previously wouldn't have bothered him in the slightest, such as speaking at my wedding or going to work. He became quiet and would only talk when he was asked a direct question. He lost interest in his hobbies and spent all his time sitting in the kitchen, watching Mum, or me when I visited. His memory started to fail. To be fair, it had always been pretty shoddy, but it became noticeably worse. Names, dates, situations all escaped him. He became shaky on his feet, unsure of his footing.

By the time he made his last film, *Snow White and the Huntsman*, in 2011, around the time he was diagnosed, these problems had all become evident. The other actors in the film looked after him with great care, particularly Ray Winstone. I will for ever be grateful to Ray for watching out for Dad and supporting him through such a terrible time.

As I said, I had a suspicion all was not well with Dad for

months prior to his diagnosis, but I suppressed it. The thought that there could be anything wrong with him was terrifying.

Before we received the official diagnosis, he was subjected to a hard-hearted procession of unpleasant tests, scans and examinations to try to determine the nature of the mysterious enemy that seemed to be taking him over. Test after test would come back with an inconclusive result, and he'd have to trek back to hospital and start all over again. He was luckier than many because he was able to afford private healthcare. But shorter waiting lists and nicer wallpaper didn't shield us from unfolding devastation.

On 28 October 2011, Mum and Dad sat Jack, Pete and me down in their kitchen and told us he had been diagnosed with Lewy body disease, an aggressive degenerative disease, and he only had a few years to live, five at the most. There was no cure and no treatment; he would lose control of his body and his mind.

Our world shattered. Dad stared down at his feet as we cried. I did my best to be strong, but it was impossible. The rest of that evening is a blur. I remember holding his hand, telling Mum that Peter and I loved her and would be there for her, and hugging my brother. But precise details are clouded by shock and anguish.

Pete and I were living in a flat that was a half-hour stroll from my folks' house. I couldn't face getting on a bus, so we walked. I sobbed every step of the way. People turned and stared but I had no control. The tears would not subside: my dad was dying.

At the time I was working backstage in a West End musical. Over the coming days I called in sick and spent much of my time at Mum and Dad's house. We went for walks in the autumn sunshine, although such simple pleasures were becoming increasingly difficult for Dad. I remember the fortitude etched into his face: it was a simple task and he fought to achieve it, but the effort really took it out of him. When we got home, he sank into a kitchen chair while I made him a cup of tea. He looked as if he had just climbed a mountain. Mum and I then went to the shops to get some food for dinner, to the pharmacy to collect the new drugs he'd been prescribed, and ran a couple of other errands. When we returned to the house about ninety minutes later, Dad was sitting in the exact same spot. He clearly hadn't moved. When he had been well, Dad overflowed with a fizzing energy; there was no way he would have sat still for so long. Even when he was exhausted, he was always busy and bustling.

Looking at him sitting there, depleted, I began to understand the severity of his condition. Later that evening, over dinner, Dad looked up at me and said, 'Fuck it.' I knew what he meant: it was his way of accepting the hand that life had dealt him. I have never witnessed such incredible courage. He was sliding backwards into an abyss, but from that moment on he was determined to enjoy what little he had left. I'm sure he kept a lot of the true horror of his condition to himself – he didn't want to burden us with his fears.

Up until his diagnosis, Dad had never been ill a day in his life (apart from his South African tapeworm, that is). In 2009, a couple of years earlier, he had had a knee replacement at the Princess Grace Hospital. When I went to see him after his surgery, he was drowsy but responsive. The next day he was sitting upright, reading a book. The day after that he was up on his crutches, hopping around the room. The day after *that* he was careering through corridors, swinging his weight back and forth on the same crutches, like a tenacious metronome. Before he got to the stairwell, the nurses stopped him and ushered him back to his room, much to his annoyance. As far as Dad was concerned, he had spent quite long enough flat on his back and it was time to get moving again.

In the early stages of his illness, when he could still get around, Ray Ward would take Dad to a physiotherapist in Primrose Hill, who would try to help ease the excruciating back pain that the illness had brought with it.

Ray and Dad looked as if they'd hatched out of the same egg: both had that short, stocky build and bore the scars of a youth spent fighting. On the way back from physiotherapy, they would stop off at the Primrose Bakery, a twee little establishment which specialises in cupcakes. The Primrose Bakery is not the sort of place one might expect to find two ageing cockneys with matching broken noses. But it became a secret weekly stop-off after physio. They would sit in the kitschy, cutesy bakery, eating pink cupcakes and drinking English Breakfast tea out of vintage porcelain teacups.

They never told Mum about their clandestine teatimes. She was concerned about Dad's weight because she knew that, if he got too fat, it would become more difficult to look after him. Ray and Dad would arrive home and complain about the traffic to Mum, while hastily wiping any telltale butter cream from their chins.

During his illness, Dad and I spent a lot of time together. Every week, Mum would go to Bristol to visit her elderly mother and we didn't wish for him to be left alone. Pete and I moved into a house in December 2011, and Mum and Dad moved down the street in March 2012. I would stroll down the road to collect him. (If he walked alone, he would pass by my house and become confused.) I'd help him put on his coat, hand him his hat and wrap a scarf around his neck if it was cold out. Then I would slip my arm through his and usher him down the street. As time oozed by, it took longer and longer for us to complete the hundred-step journey.

Whenever Dad was at my house, he would sit in an armchair with a blanket over his lap, watching TV whilst I tried to write or learn lines at the kitchen table. He had hardly ever watched TV when he'd been well – it was yet another sign of his being unwell. I always found it hard to concentrate with the telly gibbering away, but being in his company was worth it. I'd make him tea and bake his favourite oat and raisin cookies. The easy intimacy we shared during those days gave me some of my most treasured memories.

The challenge, when Dad was with me, was to keep an eye on him without making him feel that I was undermining his capabilities. I was constantly worrying that he'd fall and hurt himself, so I watched him like a hawk, but out of the corner of my eye.

One day he went to the toilet off the downstairs hallway and I didn't hear anything of him for several minutes. Concerned that he had sat down and couldn't get up, I went into the hall and called out, 'Dad, are you all right in there?'

Several moments of silence slipped by.

Then, 'Yes, I'm fine.'

My anxiety started to ratchet up a few levels.

'Do you need any help?'

'No, I'm OK, thanks.'

'Do you want me to come in?' I asked.

A pregnant pause.

'Help yourself, love.'

I really did not want to hoist my father off the toilet – it would be mortifying for us both. But if he was stuck in there,

I couldn't very well leave him stranded. I cautiously eased open the toilet door and peeped through the gap.

The toilet was empty.

Alarmed, I shouted, 'Dad! Where are you?'

Another burst of dense silence.

'I'm sitting in your front room.'

I bounded into the lounge to find Dad sitting serenely in an armchair. He had walked there of his own accord and his actor's voice had travelled down the hallway, fooling me into thinking he was on the toilet. When I told him what I'd thought he called me a soppy cow, and that was that.

In his final years I saw him almost every day and I was given many opportunities to tell him how much I loved him. People often compare a slow death with a sudden one. One might argue that the chance to say everything that needs to be said is a blessing. After all, many people lose their loved ones unexpectedly and it's too late to say 'I love you' and 'goodbye'. But a time limit set on the life of a loved one can be a form of torture, and it is no less painful than the shock of a sudden loss. It's just different.

As the disease took its toll, I would often make a point of taking a seat next to Dad, placing my hand on his and telling him that I loved him. He would raise it to his lips for a gentle kiss and then hold the back of my hand to his cheek and say, 'I love you too.'

CHAPTER FOURTEEN

DAD HAD A PHONE with a big red button on it that would call a selection of mobile numbers – Mum's, mine, Peter's and Ray's – in an emergency. The only problem was that sometimes he'd press the big red button by accident. Somehow he'd always manage to raise a false alarm when I was wearing stilettos: I would receive a call and go tearing down the street in my high heels, clatter into the house, panting and panicking, and find him happily drinking a cup of tea with Mum.

'Dad!' I'd say. 'You pressed the fucking button again!'

'Oh, sorry, love . . .' he'd say with a mischievous grin.

I know he'd have pressed it by accident – he would never have wanted to worry me – but the sight of me galloping through the door like a clumsy horse seemed to amuse him.

On some occasions there was a genuine emergency. One evening in July 2012, he fell backwards down a flight of stairs and broke all of his ribs. Mum called Pete and me. We were there in a matter of seconds and found him lying on the floor of the hallway, his skin the colour of ash and in a state of profound shock. Mum called an ambulance immediately and two minutes later, two cheerful female paramedics burst in the door with their bags stuffed with medical equipment. They attempted to get him on to a stretcher, but he was too heavy for them and they needed to call for backup.

In the meantime, they attempted to fit him with a neck brace. Dad had always joked that he didn't have a neck, and that his shoulders were soldered directly on to his ears. Years before, when playing Iago opposite Anthony Hopkins in the BBC production of *Othello*, he'd been fitted with an Elizabethan ruff collar. When it was fastened on to the gap between his head and his shoulders, the thing obscured most of his face. All anyone had been able to see were his bushy eyebrows peeking out above the decorative frills of lace.

Before attempting to fit the neck brace, the paramedics took one look at Dad and one said, 'We'll need the no-neck.' They fished around in their bags and proffered a stubby brace.

The no-neck didn't fit around Dad's no-neck.

'We'll need the paediatric one.'

It was horrible, but we couldn't help sniggering. Dad still had the self-awareness to find it funny, although laughing hurt him. The backup arrived and two burly men helped to get him on to the spinal support board and strapped down his shattered body. One of the women split her trousers as she bent down and she yelped with embarrassment. She'd put on weight since she'd stopped smoking, she explained. Dad laughed again, wincing all the while.

The paramedics encased his head in a red padded head block and busied around. I sat on the bottom stair in the hallway, gazing down at him. He didn't once break eye contact with me. Looking at me upside down must have been strange, watching as tears rolled up my face. I made a desperate effort not to cry, but I was powerless to stop it. After he was fastened to the board, the paramedics lifted him on to a gurney and wheeled him out into the blue-flashing night. Mum followed, clutching the plastic bag with his medication in it, a pink cardigan draped over her small shoulders.

Dad was out of hospital after a week, but the fall had been a significant setback. He was never the same after all his ribs smashed.

In August 2012, Dad formally announced his retirement from acting. His agent, Lindy King, released a statement telling the world Dad would no longer work because he had been diagnosed with Parkinson's disease:

> He wishes to thank all the great and brilliant people he has worked with over the years, and all of his fans who have supported him during a wonderful career.

Bob is now looking forward to his retirement with his family, and would greatly appreciate that his privacy be respected at this time.

The announcement specified that he had Parkinson's, because that was the diagnosis we had at the time. It would go on to change again. I think there was an outpouring of support from friends and well-wishers, but I don't remember much about it. My focus was solely on my parents and I shut everything else out.

The public announcement made it seem as though there was an element of choice. The truth is, if it had been up to Dad, he never would have stopped working. He might have been picky about the jobs he took in older age, but he never would have quit working altogether. Although he knew full well that he was no longer capable of doing his job, he dearly missed work. Later, when he became more confused, he'd look around the house, asking Mum, 'Where's the script?'

In the later stages of Dad's career, he chose projects that he found interesting. He'd done well-paid jobs that offered him financial security and allowed him to take care of his family. He began to take chances on new talent.

In 1996, a relatively unknown 24-year-old short-film director called Shane Meadows asked Dad to star in his first feature film, an urban drama called *Twenty Four Seven*. Set in a typical working-class town in the north of England, *Twenty*

Four Seven tells the story of Alan Darcy (played by Dad), a man who tries to get the local youths off the streets and involved in something positive: boxing. Darcy teaches them control, but he loses control of himself and beats another man to a pulp. He leaves town, only to be found years later, living rough, by one of the members of the boxing club.

Twenty Four Seven was a left-field success story, winning the Critics' Award at the Venice Film Festival and earning Shane Meadows a reputation. He went on to make *Dead Man's Shoes* and *This is England*.

I can remember when Shane came to our house for dinner – I was thirteen at the time. I don't remember too much about that evening, although I do recall Shane joking about his squat feet, insisting they are as wide as they are long.

Shane Meadows credits Dad with a large part of his early success. Not only did Dad take a huge chance on him when he agreed to star in his first feature film, but he taught Shane much about the business: how to survive it and how to stay true to yourself. 'He's the most generous actor I have ever worked with,' he says.

During the promotional tour of the film, Shane and Dad travelled together to New York. Mum, Jack and I went along too. The film company put us into first class and Shane in economy. Dad wasn't having any of it. He refused to go unless the film company either upgraded Shane to first class or downgraded him to economy. Unsurprisingly they upgraded Shane, who has never forgotten it, he says. 'Knowing he would have forgone the champers and flambé steak to sit in twerp class to me says it all, really.'

In 2000 Dad received a call from Australian director Fred Schepisi, asking if he would like to be in his adaptation of Graham Swift's Booker Prize-winning novel *Last Orders*. It's a story, set in the 1980s, about four friends who travel from London to Margate to scatter the ashes of a fifth, Jack. The cast Schepisi assembled included Tom Courtenay, David Hemmings and Ray Winstone, with Michael Caine taking on the role of Jack, who appears in flashback. Helen Mirren played Jack's long-suffering wife Amy.

I visit Ray Winstone to talk about his time working with Dad. Ray Ward drove up to the gate of his house in the country. Of course we go to the wrong entrance, and when we press the buzzer there is no answer.

I call Ray on my mobile and his warm, gravelly voice answers, "Ello, Rosa darling. You 'ere?'

I tell him I've pushed the buzzer and nothing's happened. There are a few moments of kerfuffle as he tries to get the automatic gates to open. I can hear him muttering both on the phone and on the other side. Eventually, the gates open and we head up the Winstones' driveway.

Ray stands at the door wearing a polo shirt, a pair of pink floral swimming shorts and a jovial grin. He welcomes me into his home and I ask why he's limping.

'I've broken my fucking foot,' he says.

There is a reassuring ease that comes with Ray's straightforward assessment of things, swear words that pepper most sentences, and the warmth that radiates from him reminds me of Dad. He ushers me into his kitchen and hobbles around, making cups of tea.

The family's little black dog gets overexcited at the presence of a visitor and jumps on to the kitchen table. Ray looks at the dog in mock outrage, his commanding voice booming across the kitchen: 'Oi! What do you think this is?'

The beast scampers from the table and retreats down to the floor.

Ray lights up a cigarette as we natter. Although I haven't met him before, I feel as though I've known him for years. There's a certain down-to-earth attitude that I feel comfortable with – it reminds me of Dad and his side of the family. Dad never minced his words. He would say what he thought even if it wasn't tactful or sensitive, but you always knew where you stood with him.

Over the years I've developed an aversion to passive-aggressive behaviour. People who refuse to say what they really feel but make their emotions known with spiteful silence and insipid, snide remarks are intolerable. I've become more confrontational and prepared to have uncomfortable conversations in order to avoid the trap of unsaid resentment. I find that I am more comfortable around people where the tension of unsaid truths does not exist. The Bob Hoskinses and Ray Winstones of this world don't waste their time on passive-aggression. They say what they mean and mean what they say.

Ray thinks Dad understood *Last Orders* more than anyone else in the cast. 'I don't mean any disrespect to any of the others,' he says, 'but they were playing parts. Bob somehow knew what the narrative of the film was and it was him that made it work.'

He tells me stories that I've never heard before. Apparently the pair of them caused some real mischief at Pinewood Studios. One night they were sitting in the canteen. Dad approached Ray and told him, 'If you make out it's somebody's birthday, you get a free bottle of champagne in the restaurant.' Tom Courtenay wasn't there at the time – he came along later – so they pretended it was his birthday so they could get the free bottle after dinner. Then Ray and David Hemmings took it a step further: to emphasise that it was Tom's birthday, they looked through the paper to find a strippergram.

Later, after dinner, Tom Courtenay was sitting with the others, hankies hanging out of his collar so that he didn't get make-up on his shirt, and the rest of the cast started to sing 'Happy Birthday'. All of a sudden a girl walked in, dressed up as a nurse. ('And you've got to remember, there are all these old-style producers in there too . . .') She walked past the table, did a double take, and asked, 'Excuse me, are you Mr Tom Courtenay?'

Tom said, 'Yes, I am.'

'Me and my mother love you,' she told him.

'Ooh, thank you very much . . .'

Ray laughs: 'And then she went *bosh!* and thrust her thrup-pennies all over him and he went bright red . . . We got banned from Pinewood restaurant,' he adds. 'They wouldn't let us in there after that. Bob loved that sort of thing.'

As well as being the instigator of on-set jokes, Dad was once the butt of them. He hated signing autographs – he'd often refuse point-blank if someone asked him in the street. Once when they were filming in Margate, a large group of autograph hunters crowded around the key cast members, who took one look at each other and dashed off, leaving Dad in the middle of them. 'We just left him roasting,' says Ray, 'and the last thing we heard was "You bastards!"'

Ray also worked with Dad on *Snow White and the Hunts-man* and this was when he started to notice that something was wrong. The year before, he'd been working on a film called *Ashes*, playing a character with Alzheimer's. He'd met many people through that job and had done a lot of research on the disease. 'I looked one day at Bob,' he tells me, 'and I went, fuck, the lights went out. The Bob I knew, the light had gone out. He couldn't find his feet or get from A to B so well. And there's a thing with them kind of diseases – you just become very vague.'

Ray noticed it, and Johnny Harris, who was playing Dad's character's son, noticed it too. Ray and Johnny kept quiet about it. 'I've gotta say,' Ray says, 'something like that, thank God he went quick – I mean that in the nicest possible way – rather than waking up every morning, don't know who you are, don't know who your family are, people you love and all that. It's a harsh thing to say,' he admits, 'because you're always praying something will be found.'

I don't find Ray's words harsh at all. Although Dad didn't have Alzheimer's, there are similarities between it and Parkinson's. Dad is no longer suffering and he was spared decades of horrible illness. It is a great comfort. I'm glad he had Ray Winstone and Johnny Harris looking out for him on his last job.

Another of Dad's later performances was in *Mrs Henderson Presents*, a comedy directed by Stephen Frears and written by Martin Sherman. Stephen Frears had spotted Dad's comic potential almost forty years earlier when he saw him play Queen Victoria with the Ken Campbell Roadshow upstairs at the Royal Court. 'He was just brilliant, this wonderful, funny silhouette,' Frears remembers. A few years later, he saw Dad hold his own opposite John Gielgud in *Veterans*: 'There was one particular scene in which he was absolutely hilarious.'

Dad played Vivian Van Damm, a theatre impresario who is as high-spirited and stubborn as his benefactress, Mrs Laura Henderson (Judi Dench). Based on the life of the real Mrs Henderson, the film tells the story of an eccentric, seventy-year-old, recently widowed aristocrat who buys the run-down Windmill Theatre in London's West End, to run as a hobby. She appoints Vivian Van Damm to run the place and suggests to him that they add female nudity into the equation. This is unparalleled in the 1930s Britain of the film. The Windmill is the only theatre in London allowed to remain open during the Blitz, on account of the fact that its auditorium is below street level and its shows are an essential boost for the morale of the troops who visit.

Mrs Henderson and Mr Van Damm frequently clash and squabble, but also show great affection for each other. The film's closing credits explain that, on her death in 1944, the real Laura Henderson bequeathed the Windmill Theatre to Vivian Van Damm.

Mrs Henderson Presents did well at the box office and received a total of twenty-six award nominations, amongst them four BAFTA nominations, two at the Academy Awards, three at the Golden Globes and eight British Independent Film Award nominations.

Dame Judi Dench very kindly invites me to visit her home out in the countryside. Ray Ward drives me there on a crisp, bright winter's day. Sunlight bounces off the wet rural roads. Ray doesn't like to use satnav so we spend twenty minutes reversing down driveways and lanes and turning around and around until eventually we arrive at Dame Judi's beautiful old house.

She comes to the door with arms open and a genial smile on her face. 'Darling!' she says. 'Thank you so much for coming to see me!'

I protest that it is she who is doing me the favour, but she's having none of it.

Coffee is brewed and dainty Florentine biscuits are arranged on a china plate. A little white dog snuffles around our feet in hopes of a treat. I help myself to a couple of Florentines and Judi offers me another.

'I've already had two,' I say.

'Oh, I think you could manage another,' she replies with mischief.

I've met Judi only once before, during the filming of *Mrs Henderson Presents*. She barely knew me, but now she welcomes me into her home like an old friend.

We settle in her small study crammed with mementoes of a long and illustrious career. She asks with quiet and calm concern about Dad's illness. I tell her how it took a grip of his faculties, one by one, until eventually he passed away. Her smile fades as she sits stock-still, paying close attention to my every word. Her piercing blue eyes glisten with tears, and at one point I think she might cry. It is in this moment, seeing Judi's face alive with compassion and humanity, I realise why she is one of the finest actors in the world. An array of emotions travel through her, without her making a single movement.

After a moment's silence she quietly states, 'He's the last person – and obviously this is a stupid thing to say – but he's the last person you could possibly expect something like that could happen to.'

I scrabble to change the subject. If Judi sheds even one tear I will be a snivelling heap within seconds.

I ask about the first time she came into contact with Dad. When she was cast in *Mrs Brown*, Billy Connolly told her, 'We've already cast Bob Hoskins as Queen Victoria,' and showed her a photograph (from the Ken Campbell Roadshow) of Dad as Queen Victoria. 'And I believed it for a bit,' says Judi. 'I thought, Oh, I'm miffed. So I went into *Mrs Brown* feeling a bit second-hand.' Then they worked together with Stephen Frears on *Mrs Henderson*, an experience she describes as 'glorious'.

There's a devilish twinkle in Dame Judi's eyes that speaks of delicious mischief. Dad had that exact same twinkle. He too could never resist a rude joke or naughty, politically incorrect banter. Dad and Judi were both consummate professionals, but that didn't get in the way of having a raucous good time.

Judi recalls a scene that was particularly fun to film, in which she and Dad dance on the roof of the Windmill during a bombing raid. 'I've got such a wonderful memory of dancing with Bob on that roof,' she tells me, 'doing a little kind of – oh, God! – doing that dance all over the roof, and laughing.'

Because she has very small feet, Dad said to her, 'You haven't got feet – you've got hooves!' It has become a bit of a legend in her family.

They spent a long time on that roof dancing, and Judi remembers they danced very well together. 'And there's a wonderful thing about Bob's height,' she says. 'You know, it's very rare in the movies that you can kiss somebody on the level. There have only been two actors in my life that I have been able to do that with: one is Dustin Hoffman and the other is Bob. I'm always raised up on a little bit of something. I could have kissed him all day.

'So we just had a blissful time,' she adds. 'It was blissful. The feeling on set was very, very infectious and everybody had a really nice time. It was very, very joyous. I suppose it was filming and I suppose it was work, but it didn't seem like it. And it's not often you can say that.'

Judi is the kind of old-school actor who's now becoming an endangered species. After delving into Dad's career, I realise how much of his time he spent in the theatre and that he was actually quite the luvvie. He adored the camp *joie de vivre* of theatre and frequently referred to the laughs he'd had back in his repertory days. As Judi and I talk about Dad I remember that he was a fully fledged member of the theatrical old school.

Judi and Dad shared an instant chemistry. 'I'm always saying this,' she explains. 'It's not absolutely necessary that you have chemistry with another actor, because you can make chemistry. But on the occasions you find you actually do have chemistry, believe me, the audience picks up on it. Oh God, how we laughed and laughed.' They connected straight away. 'You have actors in your mind and you grade them in a way,' she tells me. 'I mean, Bob was so extraordinary in everything he played. You wouldn't have expected there'd be so many roles he could have done but he just was able to do it. It's a sign of a really fine actor.'

Then she says, 'And people are so affectionate about him – you must have met that. You must have met incredible respect and everyone so very fond of him.'

This pattern emerges in every interview about Dad. People say more or less the same thing, only from their own perspective. His generosity, both financial and otherwise, is a running theme.

Judi insists that a generous actor makes for a better scene. There are actors who don't share the scene, she tells me: they take it, but they don't share it. So that if you're playing opposite them, you have to get in while and when you can. 'Not Bob,' she says. 'Not Bob in the slightest. There were never any histrionics.

He did the work with no fuss.' She thinks he must have found some of those scenes harder than others, but he didn't give her any indication of it. He always made room for the other actors to act and that always made the scene better. It was his personality: 'That's just the way he's put together,' Judi adds. 'And that's also what makes it so joyous because it's something that you share. It makes you want to run to work every day. So that's what I call a really good actor. Oh, we had a most marvellous time doing it.'

Our meeting draws to a natural end, and I gaze out of the window at Judi's lovely garden. I compliment her on its beauty and she points out the trees that she's planted in memory of departed friends.

'I'm going to put one in for Bob. I thought an oak might be good.'

'We're having oak leaves carved on his gravestone,' I say, and tell her about the design I drew for Dad's last memorial. Oak leaves are fitting for him: they symbolise eternal strength with the wisdom that comes from being rooted deep in the earth. I tell her that Dad always carried an acorn in his pocket whenever he was working.

Judi looks out over the garden with quiet resolve, then says, 'I'll make sure I get it planted. And next time you come down you can see it – the flourishing oak.'

· · ·

The older he became, the more Dad could pick and choose the projects that meant something to him. In 2007, he agreed to star in *Ruby Blue*, a low-budget independent film made by first-time director Jan Dunn. Jan said there were only a handful of British A-list actors that low-budget, new independent film-makers could approach – with their fingers crossed – in the hope that they would say yes, and Dad was one of them. She remembers fondly that Dad called himself 'One-take Bob': 'But I only had two weeks to shoot my film, so he met his match in me!' she laughs. 'He was absolutely fantastic. On every level, there was a warmth, a sensitivity, an intelligence. He was very creative and very funny as well.'

On such a small production, the budget couldn't stretch to a Winnebago so Jan went knocking on doors and found someone who had a camper van. She thinks Dad only ever went in it once, because he loved hanging out instead with the crew and the children that were in the film. 'He was playing games with the kids all the time, and teaching them silly songs,' says Jan. 'And *rude* songs – even when their mums were there.'

I think Dad was grateful for his career and the opportunities it afforded him. I guess because he stayed true to his roots, he knew what his life might have been without that success. Although he displayed incredible bravery and stoicism, giving up work was a huge loss for him. Chronic illness shrank Dad's world: first he gave up work, then a walk in the park became challenging, until piece by piece his body failed him and he could hardly move. But, as ever, he never complained or wasted energy dwelling on the past.

Although his mental capacities diminished every day, he was very concerned about the strain it was putting on Mum. 'He never made a fuss,' she insists. 'He was stoic in the extreme. He was never bad-tempered, and he never gave me a hard time.' Dad accepted and followed the advice given to him, and tried really hard to do the exercises the physios suggested. Mum thinks he did his absolute best to keep going as well as he could. 'And when he said he couldn't do something,' she adds, 'he really couldn't. Throughout all this he was good-natured and cheerful.'

I believe he found comfort in knowing that Pete and I lived just down the street and that we would be here for her after he was gone.

To stare down the barrel of decrepitude and death must have been appalling, but he fought back with bravery and a cheerful disposition. He still found joy and laughter in each day.

I am immensely proud of my dad for many reasons. But those final years were his finest.

CHAPTER FIFTEEN

DAD'S ORIGINAL DIAGNOSIS HAD been Lewy body disease, an aggressive strain of Parkinson's. Mum and Dad wanted a second opinion and so went to another doctor, who rediagnosed him with Parkinson's disease. However, Dad deteriorated so rapidly that Mum sought a third opinion. The last doctor determined that he had progressive supranuclear palsy, a disease with no treatment and no cure.

To mourn someone who is still alive is as perplexing as it is painful. As Dad's illness tightened its grasp, he became less present and less responsive. It felt like he was drifting away from us. We were powerless as a treacherous neurological degeneration crept up on him and robbed him of life. To watch something so insidious fell this great tree trunk of a man was heartbreaking.

He remained quiet, only talking when he was spoken to. His memory grew even worse. His speech slowed, and when asked even a simple question, his answer could take several seconds to formulate. His eyes would flicker to and fro and his brow would furrow. After what used to seem like an age, an answer would bubble to the surface: 'Yes, please, I'd love a cup of tea' or 'No, thank you, I don't want to go outside.'

He softened and became childlike. His answers were often prefaced with 'please' and followed with 'thank you'. Only on the odd occasion would the old sardonic riposte dart out: 'Of course I'm not tired of seeing you. Daft cow.'

Dad always appeared delighted whenever I showed up. Perhaps he'd have forgotten I'd already visited him several times that particular week, so my presence would come as a welcome surprise. He'd offer a gentle grin and his hazel eyes would twinkle.

In the summer of 2012 we were all caught up in London Olympic fever. Watching the athletes jump, sprint, swim and hurl themselves to medal-winning glory offered us a welcome distraction from Dad's slow demise. As he watched the Games on TV, he kept a notepad on the arm of the chair and wrote down the names of the Olympians, trying to preserve any shred of short-term recollection. At the peak of his powers, he could memorise an entire film script in an hour. The sight of him struggling to remember Usain Bolt's and Mo Farah's names would make prickly tears fall from my eyes. I'd wipe them away in haste. He didn't need me weeping and wailing.

Dad was an easy patient, cooperating with all procedures, no matter how painful or undignified. Once, on Easter Sunday 2012, I asked him if he was angry.

'What about?' he said.

'What's happening to you. Don't you feel angry?'

'Nah, fuck it. What can I do about it? There's nothing else I want to do. I just want to be here with you lot.'

'So you're at peace with it all?' I asked.

'It's the only way I can be, love.'

Dad's stoicism spurred us all on to follow his lead and squeeze every ounce of cheer out of every day. Just because Dad was ill, we never skipped any family celebration. Birthdays, anniversaries and Christmas all continued with as much joviality as we could muster. I'm so glad that we all made every effort to be happy – I would hate to think Dad's final years were spent in miserable, emotional destitution. We could still all have a good laugh together and Dad would smile from ear to ear.

The challenge of caring for someone with a serious degenerative disease is immense. It's a continual and ultimately doomed uphill battle. I watched my tiny mother fight to keep Dad as healthy as she possibly could. Sometimes I could see her physically bend beneath the turmoil that was piled upon her shoulders. She was determined never to show Dad how much his illness was affecting her. Dad still worried about her, though, and once in a while he would ask me if I thought she was doing OK. I'd reassure him because I too didn't want to expose him to any negativity.

Before Dad became ill, I had always assumed that he was the strong one. Although he'd gone bananas over a coffee pot once in a while, if the proverbial shit hit the fan, he'd held it together and provided unshakeable support. Like during the periods when I had been mentally ill: he had been there in a flash, ready to do whatever it took to get me well again.

I remember a particular occasion when my parents lived in a house that backed on to Alexandra Park. One evening I'd been heading up to see them but I caught the wrong bus. I found myself stranded outside Alexandra Palace. The place was deserted, and the park poorly lit. I called Dad in a panic.

'Don't move,' he'd said. 'I'll be there in a minute.'

Their house was a three-minute drive from where I was. Dad was there in one. I heard his engine screaming in the distance. The noise became deafening, as he thundered around the corner, driving at breakneck speed and flying over the speed bumps. His green Audi screeched to a halt. I clambered in and we zoomed off, as though we were robbing a bank.

During his illness, Mum was just as resilient as Dad. She went from being the wife of a film star to being the carer of a terminally sick man. The change was stark and bleak. Not only was she losing her husband, but she was also losing the life they had shared. Nonetheless, she was resolute.

The illness descended in deep troughs. Something would change and we would get used to a new level of disability, then there would be another dip and again he would stabilise. With each new phase, Mum would up the amount of support she gave him. She worked herself to the bone to keep him as well and happy as possible – a tiny hero in a cashmere cardigan.

As Dad always said, not everyone has a Linda.

Eventually Dad started to suffer frequent bouts of pneumonia. He was in and out of the Princess Grace Hospital from February 2014, until his last stay in April. Mum and I would traipse into the hospital every day to be by his side. Our propensity to talk the hind legs off a donkey came in useful: the hours spent with the beeping machines and Dad's rattling breath was cushioned by our comfortable companionship. Hopefully Dad didn't mind listening to us witter on about this and that for hours at a time.

I tried to carry on working, followed around by a black cloud, which wasn't just the squally February weather. London Fashion Week came and went. I spent the duration oscillating between the superficial gloss of the catwalk and the brutal reality of watching Dad's futile fight with a terminal illness. The hospital staff would gawk as I'd clack down the corridor in a variety of inappropriate outfits and impossibly high heels. I'm over six foot in heels. To them, I might as well have been dressed as a clown.

I was so relieved when the fashion circus left town and I could blend into the background again, just concentrate on being with Dad. I would hold his hand and gaze into his eyes whenever he opened them. He lost the ability to blink, so if his eyes opened, they'd stay open. They'd become red and dry so we'd moisten them with eye drops every half-hour. Sometimes he'd open his eyes and we'd hurry into his line of sight, anxious to squeeze out every last drop of contact. He'd smile when he saw Mum and me, but after a while his eyes would look so sore that I'd place drops in them and gently close them. Having his eyes forced open for minutes at a time must have been excruciating.

A few days before he died, I was sitting by his bed in the stuffy beige room while he slept. Mum had gone out for some fresh air and I was holding the fort. As his eyes fluttered open, I hurried into his field of vision, held his hand where it rested on the thin white cotton sheets that covered his diminishing body.

'Dad, I love you so much,' I told him. 'I've always loved you. From the first moment I set eyes on you, I thought to myself, You'll do. I can't remember it, but I know it was my first thought.'

As I spoke, Dad looked straight at me, taking in what I was saying.

I kept going. 'I don't think it's possible for a daughter to love a dad as much as I love you. No matter what happens in my life, I'll carry my love with me for ever. I'll treasure it for ever. I love you.'

His eyes filled with tears.

'You're the most beautiful girl in the world,' he croaked from beneath his oxygen mask. 'I love you so much.'

For one brief moment in that stark hospital, Dad and I were at peace together.

Those were the last words he said to me.

As death slithered nearer, there were endless discussions with doctors about the best possible way to treat Dad. During all of these conversations, my mum's fortitude remained unshakeable. She spoke with eloquent clarity about her husband's condition, and her composure never broke. I, on the other hand, would dissolve into tears as the talk inevitably moved towards Dad's looming death. Mum would hold my hand as she continued to talk with polite precision.

Around Dad I could just about hold it together. I even managed to make him laugh occasionally. There were times, though, that I'd have to excuse myself and find a quiet corner of the hospital where I could weep. During these moments, it felt as though my life was being dismantled around my ears and there was nothing I could do to stop it. There's an odd phenomenon that occurs at the deathbed of a loved one, something confirmed to me by other people who've gone through a similar experience. You convince yourself that your love can save them. The human spirit clings on to false hope, no matter how futile.

I loved as hard as I could, but it couldn't save him.

On the morning of 29 April 2014, we all went to the hospital to visit Dad – Mum, me, Jack, Alex and Sarah. We're a tall bunch – I'm the shortest of Dad's kids and I'm five foot nine. Dad had often said he didn't know how he ended up with a long lot. The five of us lumbered upstairs to the beige room and arranged ourselves around Dad. A heavily pregnant palliative-care nurse came to see us. She told us she was having twins. She spent a short time examining him.

Then she ushered us into a cramped room off the corridor, where she told us that he had only hours left. 'If he were my father,' she advised, 'I wouldn't leave him.'

Her words were devastating; my heart cracked as she spoke. The only small comfort was that, for the first time since Dad had been diagnosed, we at least had a clear time frame.

The nurse told us we should try to cool him down because he had a burning fever. I asked the ward nurses for half a dozen packs of antibacterial wipes and put them in the fridge in his room. We took the cold wet wipes and placed them on his brow and on his arms. After a couple of hours, his temperature dropped to a more comfortable level. He descended into a state of dying serenity. We all drew close and uttered every last unspoken word, every expression of love and every funny story. We formed a circle around him and bathed him in words of affection.

As the day wore on, we grew tired and ordered some food. I had a slab of croque-monsieur, which was horrid. I forced down a mouthful and left the rest.

The room was stuffy and dim and we all sat on chairs around the edges of the bed. I had nothing else to say but I didn't want him to die in silence. So I sat next to him, stroked his brow and sang all his favourite songs. I sang every one, gently and quietly: his final lullaby. The last song was 'Wolfcry'. As I sang, his breath grew more ragged and laboured but I kept on singing. I was resolute. He was there when I came into the world, and I was there as he left it.

After Dad slipped away, Mum stood over his lifeless body. 'What a blessed soul,' she said. 'He fought so hard and we loved him so much. God bless him.'

Her compassion and kindness were remarkable. She was devastated that her soulmate had died, but she was relieved that he had been released from suffering.

Again and again, throughout the day, Mum had told Dad that he was 'loved and adored'. These were the words she used throughout the years of his illness to let Dad know he was her beloved. He'd smile beneath his oxygen mask and his eyes told her that she was loved and adored too.

CHAPTER SIXTEEN

On 30 June 2014 we bury Dad's ashes. It seems as if every time we perform ceremonial rites of passage, the sun shines. As Mum, Alex, Sarah, Jack and I make our way to the cemetery, sunlight cascades through the trees, illuminating the gravestones.

Alex's partner, Jane, and his little two-year-old daughter come with us too. Dad met Ellie a few times before he died. I'm glad that he met at least one grandchild. He was too ill to play with her the way he did with us when we were little. When you lose a loved one, you're deprived of not only their presence in your world, but your future together. It breaks my heart that Dad will never meet my children.

We are greeted at the gate by the sexton, a gentle giant called Victor. He has enormous hands and a sensitive, kind disposition. He's holding a cardboard box about the size of a shoebox. He opens the lid to reveal a small wooden casket, with a brass nameplate, inscribed:

ROBERT WILLIAM HOSKINS

26.10.1942 to 29.04.2014

It's surreal that my dad, a looming presence, a pivotal figure in my life, is reduced to a little box of dust.

We walk to the grave Victor has prepared for the burial. He takes Dad out of his cardboard box and hands Jack the casket. Jack has the same stocky build as Dad, only taller. He has the same hazel eyes and the same grin. Jack is very creative and artistic; he loves to make things with his hands. He has a lot of Bob senior's talent.

Jack slowly places Dad in the ground and we all take a shovel and cover the box with earth until the hole is filled. Sarah reads a passage from the *Tao Te Ching* by Lao-Tzu – Dad gave each of us a copy years ago. The *Tao Te Ching*, or 'Book of the Way', is an ancient Chinese philosophical text filled with useful advice on how to live well. In Dad's later years he became very interested in Eastern religion.

Ellie is good as gold and waits in her pushchair, observing us all with quiet interest. She can't understand what's happening, but she appears to sense that this is a sombre occasion.

I want to sing 'Amazing Grace'. I take a deep breath and a knot of grief swells in my throat and strangles my voice. I try again. This time, the sound comes out clear and loud. I had intended to sing a soft rendition of the hymn but if I try to temper the volume I'll crack. My only option is to belt it out at the top of my lungs. A flock of birds take flight, alarmed by the klaxon of my voice.

We linger around the grave for a while to say our good-byes. It's strange how there are shades of finality. The moment he died, the funeral, and now this. It still doesn't feel like the end, but this is his last stop where he will lie for ever. Dad wasn't particularly religious, but he had spiritual inclinations. It's difficult to say exactly what they were: his take on the world was so original it's impossible to pigeonhole him. When I interviewed him, we spoke about spirituality and he recited a prayer he'd written years before:

I am what the world has made me,
And yet a brief interlude of tenderness can transform
    this twisted soul,
Even I am overwhelmed by the extent of my gratitude.

It's time to leave and we wander out of the cemetery, through dappled light filtered by the leaves of ancient trees.

We go home and eat. Mum has put on a big spread: pasta with home-made tomato sauce, plates of Parma ham, a few different salads, cheese and hunks of bread. Dad would approve.

We're a family of feeders. Nearly all of the significant events in my family have culminated in gathering around the table, pouring wine and eating together. I remember one meal in particular, in the summer of 2012, during the Olympics. It was a balmy evening and we ate outside. I cooked spaghetti and meatballs, one of Dad's favourites. I mixed pork and beef to make them extra succulent and tasty. The tomato sauce bubbled away for a long time to intensify the flavour. For dessert, I simmered summer berries with a vanilla pod, sugar and a splash of elderflower cordial and served them with tennis-ball-sized scoops of vanilla ice cream.

When we were done, Dad said, 'I could eat all of that again.'

These days I cook healthier food, but while Dad was still alive I was keenly aware that our mealtimes were precious. I made the crowd-pleasing dishes I knew he loved. Now, whenever I strain piping-hot pasta at the sink, I'm reminded of the meals Dad cooked for us when we were kids.

Birthdays and anniversaries have been some of the hardest times, when I feel his loss the most. Dad's seventy-second birthday has been looming on the horizon. He didn't make a big deal of his birthday, but he saw it as a great excuse to have a piece of cake and a glass of champagne. It was difficult to buy him presents. He wasn't particularly materialistic; he liked books, music and cameras. The trouble was, if he saw something he wanted in a magazine or online, he'd jump in his car and buy it there and then. I would buy him CDs and books that I thought he'd like and he'd open them and smile politely, but I think he already had most of what I bought him.

On his seventieth birthday, I baked him a vanilla sponge with green icing – his favourite colour. Unfortunately, I over-estimated my baking skills: the sponge came out flat and dense and the pale green icing spilled over the edge like insipid lava. The thing looked like a giant had sneezed on to the plate. I hastily ordered a cake from the Primrose Bakery, which was a lovely shade of green and had 'Happy Birthday Bob' expertly piped across the top. I knew his birthdays were limited and couldn't bear the thought of the snot cake being his last.

We're going to the cemetery again today to light candles and wish him a happy birthday.

When we get there, Mum, Jack and I stand, our arms around each other, in silent contemplation. I feel his presence in the trees and the falling scarlet and amber leaves. I watch the candles flicker among the flowers planted on his grave. I imagine him tapping his foot impatiently, waiting for us to show up with candles and cake.

It's peaceful to stand in silence, surrounded by gravestones. Other mourners tend the graves of their loved ones. The community of grave-owners are respectful of one another, bounded by a common loss. A woman walks past us to the grave of a little boy and potters around, weeding and removing the slugs that encroach on the memorial of her child.

Without warning, I feel an eruption of burning fury. I want to scream, to rage at the universe. I want to tear everything apart – the graves, the trees, the very earth itself. I have an urge to lie down on the grass next to Dad's grave and sink down into the earth beside him. I realise lying on the ground is morbid and would upset Mum and Jack. It would also be at odds with the stranger down the way whose grief is quiet and dignified.

Then I have a flashback: an image of when Dad gasped his last breath as I sat inches away from him. The most traumatic event of my life replays again and again in my mind. It darts across my vision, uninvited. Sometimes I wake up in the night, drenched in sweat. At other times it visits me during the day. The vision drags me back to the acute pain I was in at the moment he died. I try to shake it off and return to the present but these flashbacks are beyond my control. I've stumbled through the past six months, wrapped up with Dad's memory. The process of writing about him has blurred my working life with my personal life, resulting in a murky puddle of grief. I'm having nightmares and jolting awake several times every night.

CHAPTER SEVENTEEN

MY BEST FRIEND IS getting married tomorrow in Kent and I'm to be one of half a dozen bridesmaids. I know leaving the house will be a challenge as I'm experiencing regular panic attacks, which are exacerbated by having to deal with the day-to-day business of the outside world. I feel foolish about being so jumpy, so vulnerable. After all, I'm not a war veteran or a fleeing refugee. I witnessed the death of my father, not genocide. I hate myself for this.

Pete has to coax me through the door and out of the house, gripping my hand and muttering words of comfort. My composure is just about intact as we make our way to the tube station, wheelie suitcase clattering behind us. Suddenly Dad is here at the moment of death. I grab a sharp breath as the panic strains at its shackles. Pete holds my hand and leads me down on to the platform. The train comes bellowing along the tunnel and I have a sudden urge to jump.

Pete guides me on to a carriage and keeps talking, helping me hold it together. The carriage is crowded and noisy. My heart races and sweat beads on my palms. At Victoria station we head up the escalators. Dad's here again, stricken and dying. I'm flooded with grief.

The frenetic concourse is like being inside a swarm of bees. Panic rises from my stomach; I feel it tighten in my throat. I'm hyperventilating. Along with the tidal wave of desperate hysteria, I'm also filled with self-loathing. Why am I so weak? Why can't I get on a train like a normal person? But I can't. I can't get on and we miss the train.

Dinner is being served at the hotel for the guests arriving the night before the wedding. I know my friend will be wondering where I am, but I'm rooted to the spot. As I sit on a bench with Pete, he tries his best to calm and mollify me. I'm starting to lose control of my speech and I'm stuttering. He gives me a bottle of water and I take a few sips. We wait until the next train pulls on to the platform and we board, although walking through the station is terrifying. I feel smothered by the constant disembodied announcements and frenzied surge of commuters. To me, Victoria station resembles a scene painted by Hieronymus Bosch. If the bride were not such a dear friend, I would turn around right now and run home. But I must get there for her.

We clamber on to the train but all seats are taken. Pete ushers me into a corner of the carriage and commands me to sit on the suitcase. I turn my back on the other travellers and bury my head in my hands. Here's Dad again, dying, dead.

When we arrive at our destination, assuming there will be a taxi rank, instead we're greeted by a dark, empty street. Now I really start to fall apart. I'm trembling and unable to control the sounds coming out of my mouth. I yelp like a distressed puppy. Pete phones the hotel and arranges for a cab to pick us up. We wait about forty minutes; there's only one taxi driver and he's on another job. We've missed most of dinner. I hope my friend will understand.

Eventually, the taxi arrives to collect us from the gloomy street and we make a winding journey to the hotel. The tide of panic is starting to subside, although I'm still shaking and yelping. We cruise through the shadowy grounds of the country-house hotel, lit only by the glow from its windows. I'm too embarrassed to approach the reception, as I still haven't regained complete control of myself. I see one of the other bridesmaids standing outside on the terrace, smoking a cigarette, and the turmoil starts to rise once more. It's impossible for me to walk into a dining room full of guests. Peter goes into the hotel and checks us in. I stand outside, immovable.

I realise it will be considered rude if Pete and I don't show our faces in the dining room, where the other guests are now finishing their meal. I do my best to choke back the anxiety. It feels as if I'm trying to swallow a live mouse.

We walk in and, luckily, the bride is sitting near the door. She spots my distress and ushers us into the room next door, where there is the remainder of a buffet. She reassures me and Pete and I load our plates with tepid food and take them to our room.

Now we're safely locked away, I begin at last to calm down. I still feel the anxiety bubbling in my stomach but the worst of the panic attack has passed. I can nibble at the food and I hang up my bridesmaid's dress so that the creases can drop out. I lie down on the bed; it's comfortable. I drift into unconsciousness, but again I'm jolted awake in the night by the vision of Dad on his deathbed.

I wake up tired and agitated; it's the six-month anniversary of Dad's death. I know I have to put on a good front today. Pete and I find our way to the bridal suite, where my friend and some of the other bridesmaids are milling around, drinking coffee and eating croissants. Pete stays for a few minutes and then excuses himself – this is a women-only zone and he feels out of place. He tells me to text him if I need him. I'm feeling calmer, though I know my composure is precarious. I make conversation with the others about this and that as the room starts to fill up with people: a couple of hairdressers, a make-up artist for the bride, the mother of the bride, the mother-in-law and the last two bridesmaids. I feel hot panic begin to rise again from my stomach and creep towards my throat.

I'm yanked back in time – six months – to that stuffy room in the Princess Grace Hospital. The feeling is so visceral I let slip a small, smothered howl. I have to get out. I tell the bride that I'm going to write my blog. I should probably come up with a better excuse, but I don't have time. I have to escape this crowded, noisy place.

Back in our room, I find Pete lying on our bed, reading a book. I want to cry, but if I let go now I'll never make it through the day. Instead, I scream into a pillow for a minute or two. Pete strokes my back and whispers, 'It's all OK.' I don't believe him. I tell him that the bride seems peeved. He reasons that it's a Wednesday, a working day for most people, and stepping out briefly is not unreasonable. I re-manacle my angst and decide to go ahead and write my blog. Writing focuses my attention. Twenty minutes later, I've finished my work and have organised my facial features into a joyful, wedding-friendly arrangement. I return to the bridal suite.

When I re-enter, the room is full of excited chatter and laughter. Hopefully no one will notice that there's anything wrong with me. Champagne is passed around; I take a glass and busy myself doing the other bridesmaids' make-up. I consider telling someone what's going on but I know that if I let the mask slip, even for a second, my terror and grief will spill out in a messy heap. I can't allow this. This is not the appropriate time or place to weep over my dead dad. Considering the turmoil I'm going through, I think I'm putting on a convincing front.

Eventually the time comes to walk down the aisle. The bride, her father, the five other bridesmaids and I make our way to the function room where the ceremony is to take place. Everyone's attention is on my best friend. She looks beautiful. No one notices the convulsing muscle in my jaw, grinding at my teeth.

It's a lovely ceremony, but I can't connect with the present. I feel as if I'm floating over the room, observing it all through the glass window of the beige room in the Princess Grace. The ceremony ends and I make my way to the reception. I head straight to Peter, who grips my hand and quietly asks if I'm OK. A tiny shake of the head tells him no, I'm not.

We go about the business of greeting the other guests, congratulating the couple and drinking more champagne. I'm starting to relax a little. By dinner time the alcohol blurs the edges of the stampede tearing through my chest. I chat, joke and laugh at all the appropriate moments. I ask one of the bridesmaids for a cigarette; smoking is a good excuse to stand outside in the drizzling rain and breathe deeply. I'm not usually a smoker and it makes me feel a little sick. Back inside, the room starts to spin. I realise I have two choices: I can drink my way through this thing and get steaming drunk, or I can stay sober and relatively in control. I opt for the latter.

Although the thought of drinking my feelings away is tantalising, I've used alcohol to self-medicate in the past, when I've felt uncomfortable in social situations, and it led to nothing but mess.

I switch to water and sobriety catches up with me.

The speeches come and go, people saying touching, funny things about the couple. Again I have a strange sensation of floating above my body, looking down on the proceedings. I want to be in the room, to be present and focused on my best friend's wedding, but I can't. Looming post-traumatic stress has me wrapped up in a straightjacket. I hope no one notices that my laugh is fake.

The couple take their first dance. They glide across the dance floor, a picture of elegance. Everyone is smiling – they seem happy. I wonder if anyone else is wearing a mask.

After a while, Pete says that he's off to bed, that he's tired. I sometimes forget that looking after me must take it out of him. Over the last few years, he's been a rock. Patient, understanding and kind, even when I've acted out and behaved poorly. I don't know what I would do without him.

I decide to stay up for a while, but I say that I will come back to the room to say goodnight to him. As the door closes behind us, the mask finally drops and I start to cry. Mascara runs down my face in sooty streaks. There's nothing for it: I have to surrender and go to bed. It's a massive relief. At last I can let it all out. I sob on Pete's shoulder for what feels like a long time. I peel off my dress and crawl into bed. Pete murmurs that he loves me and his breath soon becomes a gentle snore. The sound of the party pounds on. It's early, about 10 p.m. A cheer rises up: someone has downed a shot or performed a funny dance move. If I weren't grieving, I would be dancing right now. I'd probably be the last to go to bed.

I wake up covered in sweat. My dying dad is lodged inside my brain like a film on a loop. The repetition does nothing to blunt the horror. All is quiet. The party is over.

In the aftermath of the wedding, it is clear I need help. The adrenalin and shock of Dad's death have worn off. The messages of condolence have dried up and everyone else is getting on with their lives. Moving on. I, on the other hand, am left with only the intolerable reality that Dad is gone for good. There will be no more hand-holding, no more 'I love you's, just a yawning void where he used to be.

CHAPTER EIGHTEEN

A COUPLE OF DAYS later, I tell a good friend what happened. He's been through a similar thing and insists that I see an EMDR therapist to deal with the post-traumatic stress disorder (PTSD). I do a little internet research and find out EMDR (eye movement desensitisation and reprocessing) is a type of psychotherapy often used in the wake of a traumatic or distressing event that can overpower the brain's coping mechanisms. During treatment, the patient focuses on the recurring event, whilst following the therapist's pen as it is waved from side to side.

Although I continue with daily life, I can't deny I'm struggling and it's getting worse. The thought of going through this terrible stuff with a therapist is not appealing, but my symptoms are intensifying.

My friend makes a few phone calls, emails me a list of therapists in my area and instructs me to contact them straight away. I procrastinate for a couple of weeks: facing the reality of what is going wrong in my head is frightening. My friend insists I get on with it. I do as I'm told. The first therapist who replies to my email is a lady called Diana. We speak on the phone. She sounds rather posh, but also warm and sympathetic. We arrange a meeting later that week.

The day comes to visit the EMDR therapist. Diana greets me when I enter the building. She's a nicely dressed, dark-haired lady in her late forties. She leads me to the treatment room, which is plainly furnished with oatmeal-coloured chairs and cream walls. There's a bland watercolour of a seaside landscape. It's comfortable nonetheless.

She sits opposite me with a clipboard and asks questions about what's brought me to her office. I tell her about the panic attacks, the nightmares and the flashbacks. She agrees I have PTSD and EMDR is the appropriate treatment. I'm not ready for the waving pen just yet; I think that will come next week.

I leave emotionally raw, but feeling empowered by having taken action. Being haunted by Dad's death is getting in the way of the natural grieving process. Hopefully Diana can help me dispense with this trauma. Ray has agreed to meet me and give me a lift home. There's a greengrocer's opposite Diana's practice selling Christmas trees. I make the impulsive decision to buy one. It's probably a bit early to buy a tree. Every year I get overexcited and buy a tree in early December, only for it to be drooping and forlorn by the time Christmas Day comes around. I decide to go for it anyway. Ray helps me pick out a towering tree. We heave it into the car and he drives me home.

The first Christmas without Dad was always going to be hard. He loved Christmas.

Like most children, Christmas was my favourite time of year. The house would twinkle with dozens of lights. In the eighties, our decorations were multicoloured – there was lots of metallic tinsel and gaudy baubles too – and our home would look like a shimmering rainbow. In the early nineties, Mum decided she'd had enough of our house looking like a Christmassy gay bar. She suggested we should limit the colour palette to red, green and gold and banned tinsel. One year, when I was about nine years old, a string of lights blew while we were decorating the tree, so she sent Dad out to buy some more. I went with him. We were given strict instructions to pick up tasteful, plain white lights.

But then Dad and I spotted a set that were irresistible – bulbs of garish colours, with each fixture shaped like a Cinderella coach. The lure of the pantomime lights proved too much for both of us. Dad, whose inner child was alive and well, bought them. Mum was not impressed when we got home.

By then, Dad and I were so attached to our illuminated

carriages that he went back out and bought a miniature Christmas tree to be decorated with the outmoded baubles. We decked it out in the Cinderella lights and pink, yellow and blue baubles of old, and stuck one of my Barbie dolls on the top. It was an affront to good taste and we loved it. These days all my Christmas decorations are tasteful and contemporary – I take after Mum in many respects – but I still have a soft spot for naff tinsel and gaudy festive knick-knacks. (The Cinderella carriage fairy lights were made by a company called Pifco and now sell for hundreds of pounds on eBay.)

When I was eleven, we decorated the house in Belsize Park with candles. Everywhere you looked, there were tea lights and tall-stemmed flames and the house flickered with a warm glow. As Christmas Day passed, we went around and blew out the burning lights, apart from one decoration in the corner that we forgot.

It was a flowerpot filled with pine cones that had been sprayed gold, dried flowers and decorative sticks of cinnamon, with two long candles poking out of its centre. They were lit in the morning and by early evening they had burned down to the base and ignited the ornamental kindling at the bottom. Jack discovered the pot with flames blazing several feet high.

Dad and Granddad were in the next room, but rather than raise the alarm with them, Jack ran to the top of the house, where Mum and I were. Mum called down to Dad to sound the alarm and we all rushed to the room. Jack, who was nine, was so used to Mum being in charge that it hadn't occurred to him to tell Dad. But Dad was great in an emergency: he went to the kitchen, dampened a tea towel under the tap, used this to protect his hands and carried the flaming pot out into the garden. He may have been prone to losing his rag over trifling incidents, but when it counted he could be relied upon to make quick decisions and fix whatever had gone wrong.

When we were little, Jack and I always woke up at the crack of dawn on Christmas Morning to see if Father Christmas had visited. My parents had usually been up until the wee small hours wrapping toys, only for us to burst into their room and holler that Father Christmas had been. They'd watch us open the presents through bleary eyes and then stumble downstairs to put the dinner on. I can remember Mum in her dressing gown, dealing with the turkey, and Dad peeling potato after potato.

As I got older, I started to help out with the cooking. My favourite part was preparing the sausage-meat stuffing: I loved squelching the cold raw pork mince through my fingers.

Both my parents were cooking enthusiasts and would go to town with the Christmas food. In the moments before the meal was served, Dad would take the long, pointed carving knife from the rack and fish out his sharpening steel. Then he would stand in the centre of the kitchen with the steel in his left hand and the blade in his right, honing the knife until it was sharp enough to split a hair. He sharpened with pomp and flourish – it was an essential part of the Christmas ceremony.

When Dad attacked the turkey, he'd stick out his tongue from the corner of his mouth and furrow his brow. In later years, once he was too ill to do it, I took over carving the bird at Christmas. The last one we had with him, he sat in the kitchen, watching me as I sliced the meat, my tongue out and my brow creased, with a knowing smile creeping across his face.

At about 11 a.m., Dad would put on *The Christmas Album* – someone gave it to us in the early nineties and we played it every single year. When we moved house in 2006, the Christmas CD was lost in transit. But I remembered every song and the compilation order, so I replicated it on my laptop. The playlist starts with 'Last Christmas' by Wham! Dad's favourite song from the album was Jona Lewie's 'Stop the Cavalry'. He used to caper around the kitchen doing a bobbing oompah dance, his shoulders rising and falling in time to the brass band. He'd sing along with Lewie's 'Dob-a-dob-a-doom-doom' like a cockney crooner.

After 'Stop the Cavalry' comes 'Merry Xmas Everybody' by Slade. Dad did a brilliant Noddy Holder impression and would holler 'It's CHRIISST-MAAAAS!' – which ratcheted our childish excitement up to fever pitch.

Around midday, Dave and Jane would come over, sometimes with their daughter Polly as well. Mum used to put out smoked salmon on rye bread, and Dad would open a bottle of champagne. I was allowed a small glass from the age of fifteen. The house was filled with jolly voices and rowdy laughter.

After Dave and Jane left, we would start work on the final stages of assembling the lunch. A Christmas meal isn't hard to cook: it's all a matter of timings. But the last half-hour is critical. One year, when I was twenty-three, I offered to cook the whole meal. Everything went very well until the last few moments. I was making gravy and Dad was hovering over my shoulder, anxious that I might mess it up. It's not that he didn't have any faith in my ability, but to him the gravy was the lynchpin of a roast dinner. Eventually I told him to bugger off – he was putting me off my game. Fortunately the gravy was a triumph and the rest of the meal was pretty good too (even if I say so myself).

Like any family, we had our traditions. One was pulling crackers and wearing the stupid paper crowns that come with them. Granddad – Bob senior – lived with us for years in the house in Belsize Park; he had a flat on the ground floor. He had an unfortunate habit of telling dreadful jokes. Every Christmas he'd offer to clear up the wrapping paper and discarded crackers. Whilst collecting the crinkled and ripped paper, he'd scavenge the cracker jokes and put them in his pocket, storing them up for the year ahead.

Towards the end of the day, we'd lie around and watch TV, usually a BBC Christmas special or a film. (I swear Christmas telly used to be much better than it is today.)

Our final Christmas with Dad was lovely, but I knew that it would be our last. In the run-up to the day I was filled with dread. I didn't want it to come. There was a savage beehive of anxiety in my stomach that I tried to ignore. I did my best to carry on with business as usual, but the slightest thing would tip me over.

A week or so before Christmas, Pete and I invited friends over for dinner. I prepared a chocolate dessert the day before. I usually find baking soothing: there's something about melting chocolate, sifting flour and whipping butter and sugar into a fluffy pale cloud that's reassuring. This time, however, I managed to drop a large bowl full of melted chocolate on to the floor. It splashed up the walls, all over the place, and I even managed to get it in my hair. I burst into tears and then felt like an idiot. Why was I crying over spilt chocolate? I scolded myself for being so stupid. In retrospect, it's clear I was a raw nerve.

Later that week, I decided to do some Christmas shopping in Selfridges. Going into battle with December crowds on Oxford Street is a fool's errand at the best of times, but I was in town for an audition so I thought I might as well. I quickly became overwhelmed and ran out of the store, bumping into several people on the way. The pavement was a manic swarm of shoppers bundled up against the cold and each other. Attempting to pass through the mob seemed as terrifying as marching through a stampede of buffalo. I scuttled behind a Christmas tree by the main entrance of Selfridges, crouched down and cried like a lost child. After ten minutes or so, I crept out from my hiding place and tentatively made my way home.

Despite weeping over chocolate and hiding behind Christmas trees, I did my best to be cheerful around Dad. I was determined that our last months with him would be as happy as possible. On 23 December, I stapled my poise back together and tried to make our last Christmas a merry one.

I cooked for hours on Christmas Eve, making cranberry sauce and performing the rather gruesome task of lifting the skin from the meat of the turkey and smearing butter all over the breast. After that, I did my favourite job of squelching the sausage-meat stuffing together with onions, sage, breadcrumbs and eggs. I made the base for the gravy. This was crucial – it had to be the best ever.

On Christmas Day I found previously unknown reserves of emotional fortitude. I compartmentalised the pain and focused on the moment. Pete and I had breakfast and then my parents and my brother came over. I set Jack to work lighting candles and ironing the 'best' tablecloth. Mum and Dad bought it in Italy many years ago when he was playing Mussolini.

We had our usual midday snack of smoked salmon and champagne. I put on the Christmas album and the bouncy intro to 'Last Christmas' by Wham! started up. We raised a glass and wished each other a merry Christmas. Dad said, 'Happy Christmas, everyone,' a few seconds after the rest of us – by then, his responses were too slow to keep up. Where once his voice had been booming and resonant, it was now a feeble croak.

Pete, Jack, Mum and I busied around the kitchen, getting the meal together and cracking jokes. Mum often darted back to Dad's side, held his hand and kissed his cheek. Since the bastard illness had gripped his faculties, his laughter had been reduced to a quiet chuckle. Nonetheless, he spent the entire day smiling. We sat down to eat – it was good and the gravy was a resounding success. Dad ate very slowly, enjoying every morsel.

Throughout the meal, I played Dad's favourite Christmas music. The first song on was 'Stop the Cavalry'. He was no longer capable of doing the dance that had once had us all in stitches, but he still sang a quiet rendition of 'Dob-a-dob-a-doom-doom'. As the brass section kicked in, a grin bloomed on his face and his eyes twinkled. He tapped out the rhythm on the table and nodded his head to the music.

I think he liked that song because it's about a man longing to go home. Although he thrived on travel, he suffered from homesickness. He was happiest at home with us. As he listened, it seemed to me all the Christmases that we had spent as a family were flashing before his eyes. (This may not be true at all – for all I know he was just enjoying the song.)

After lunch, we gathered around the tree to open presents. We had to help Dad open his gifts – CDs from Peter and me, a scarf from Mum and slippers from Jack. I took dozens of pictures – I wanted to capture every moment. My favourites are of Dad and me, sitting next to each other by the tree. We're holding hands and my eyes are filled with tears, but I'm smiling with every muscle in my face. He had just told me how he adored me and thanked me for the day.

As the day drew to a close, we helped Dad into his coat. The end of the Christmas album was playing – the last song is Bing Crosby's 'White Christmas'. As we wrapped Dad up against the bitter chill outside, the song struck a chord with him. It had been one of Granddad's favourites. Dad murmured, 'Just like the ones I used to know.' His voice was feeble, but he hit every note.

When everyone had gone home and the dishes were washed, I turned the lights out with a sigh of relief. Not only had I got through the day without breaking, but I had succeeded in hosting a happy family Christmas. Dad smiled all day, laughed and sang his favourite songs. Even though illness had stripped him of everything, his presence at that last Christmas was powerful. He sat next to the tree, admiring the lights; he enjoyed the food and the drink. He said 'Happy Christmas, everyone' and 'Thank you, my love. I had a great day.' I couldn't really have asked for much more. Christmas without Dad feels like it will never be the same again.

On Christmas Eve 2014, Jack, Mum and I head to the cemetery to carry out our new tradition of lighting candles and communing with Dad. It's a startlingly clear day. The trees are edged with a silver frost that sparkles in the sun.

We place a bunch of red roses, mixed with gold-sprayed twigs and pine cones, on his grave. It looks very festive. We stand still and silent. A robin hops on to Dad's gravestone, cocks its head and seems to regard us with interest. The scene could be lifted from a macabre Christmas card. I grope for the phone in my pocket, hoping to take a picture. The robin bursts into song and then takes off in a flurry. I manage to photograph it leaving but miss the shot I was hoping for. (I didn't inherit Dad's knack for photography.)

We stand by the grave a while longer. Time seems to lose meaning here. There is no morning, afternoon or evening. Just a still silence.

It's time to go. We all say, 'Bye, Dad. Merry Christmas,' and I run my fingers over his name etched in the stone.

Christmas Day dawns crisp and sunny – another significant moment without Dad when the sun's shining. I don't believe in spirits or an afterlife, but if I did, I'd think the sun was Dad, reminding us to enjoy life.

I wake up tired. After a strong cup of coffee, I trudge around getting ready. Mum and Jack come to our house and we clamber into a cab. Mum's booked lunch for us at a restaurant just by Tower Bridge. We've never been there before. We decided to go out on Christmas Day this year as we couldn't face a family meal at home without Dad.

We don't speak on the journey across London. I've never been out on Christmas Day before – I'm surprised by how many people are around. When we reach Tower Bridge there are groups of Japanese tourists, taking photos of the river and of themselves. We amble down the steps of the bridge and make our way to the restaurant. The place is light and airy and there's a pleasant, festive atmosphere. There are groups of families; some of them seem to be missing a member, like ours. There are a couple of women in their early seventies sitting by the window. I wonder what their story is.

A jovial waitress ushers us to our table. As soon as we sit

down, our collective mood lifts. We drink champagne, pull crackers, wear the stupid hats and tell the dreadful jokes. We raise a glass and toast to Dad. He's conspicuous by his absence, but we follow the example by which he led throughout his life, and throughout his illness. The food is pretty good, although the gravy isn't as good as mine. We smile and enjoy the meal.

When it's time to leave we step out and look at the river. Tower Bridge glimmers against the clean blue sky like cut glass. I'm reminded of a scene in *The Long Good Friday*, where Harold Shand stands on the boat and delivers a speech, framed by Tower Bridge behind him. Dad is everywhere I look, in everything I touch.

I look up at the bridge and murmur, 'Happy Christmas, Dad.'

His voice echoes in my head: 'Happy Christmas, love.'

CHAPTER NINETEEN

CHRISTMAS HASN'T BEEN NEARLY as bad as I expected but I'm glad to see the back of it. The next emotional hurdle is New Year's Eve. It's my least favourite in the round of festive celebrations; last year, Pete and I stayed in and watched TV. This time I'd like to go out – being in the house will be depressing, I think – but I'm anxious about leaving my family. When I spoke to Pete and Jack about it, they both said they would be more than happy to see New Year in quietly at home. Mum, however, shares my urge to go out.

One of my best friends, Paul, is having a party at his house in south London and he's invited us both. I'm a little nervous about bringing her. Not that I think she'll embarrass me. Since Dad became ill, we've gone out alone together a lot and she's often accompanied me to Fashion Week. Mum can be dropped into most social situations and get on famously with everyone. But this evening will be particularly tough and we are both fragile. She's concerned about being the only person over thirty-five, but Paul has reassured me that it will be a mixed crowd.

When we arrive the party is thronging with young people,

mostly Paul's friends who work with him in TV. Some of the older guests he's been expecting have cancelled. Mum scans the room and realises that she stands out like a sore thumb. We scuttle to the kitchen and I tell her that we can leave. But then Paul finds us and hands us glasses of champagne, and some of his friends come and say hello. Mum is charming and interested in these new people. Soon we both relax into the evening, and before we know it, it's midnight.

Mum has told me that she is looking forward to it no longer being 2014. I have mixed feelings about it. On the one hand, I'm eager to move past the early stages of jagged grief, but as time marches on, Dad seems further away.

The clock strikes and it's no longer 2014. Mum decides to go home but I stay on another couple of hours. I'm a bit the worse for wear by the time I stumble into a cab. My taxi passes by the Shard, illuminated and stabbing at the sky with its jagged peak. As we cross the river, I watch the reflection of London shimmering on the Thames. My identity is interwoven with this city. I've lived in north London my whole life, as did Dad, and generations of our family before him. He was a Londoner to his bones and, as I travel around my home town, I'm reminded of him at every turn. I feel his presence so strongly, I could swear he's sitting next to me in this cab.

• • •

I've now had several sessions with Diana, and the PTSD is starting to shift. We talk about the moment that's been haunting me, when Dad took his last breath. I focus in on that image, I remember all the details, I allow the horror to reside in my mind's eye. It's harrowing, but now I can face it. Then Diana waves her magic pen and I follow it with my eyes, side to side. With every session, I feel the trauma slowly lift. The invisible boulder I've been carting around is diminishing. Now I have space to grieve, without fear. It's a long, hard slog with no short cut. I cry for Dad every day, but it doesn't feel quite as desperate and raw. I suppose I'm getting used to it.

Mum and I decide it's time for a holiday. It's been too long since Mum went away; her world has revolved entirely around Dad's care for over three years.

We book into a beach resort in Bodrum on the coast of Turkey. Pete and I went there seven years ago and, unless it's changed since then, I'm sure she'll like it.

Jack, Mum, Pete and I arrive at Stansted Airport. Now Dad's gone, travelling is simpler because we don't have to factor his fame into our plans. EasyJet is the only airline that flies directly to Bodrum. We board the flying sardine can and take our seats in the front row. This affords us plenty of opportunity to people-watch. There's a wide cross section of folks boarding the plane: a group of lads on a stag do, several families with small children, a gaggle of older ladies and some very smart-looking couples toting expensive hand luggage.

I expect our first trip without Dad to be painful. He is constantly on our minds, but we're determined not to be maudlin and we enjoy the break, mostly spent lying on the beach and reading.

We talk about him every day, reminiscing about holidays past. Really, Dad would have preferred to go on sightseeing trips to historical sites, but we all wanted to lie on the beach. To be fair, it's likely that he would have been harassed by other tourists on sightseeing holidays, so it probably worked out better for him anyway. But he didn't much like the heat and used to spend most of the time in his room, reading. In the cooler parts of the day, he'd venture out with his camera and take arty shots of flowers and sunsets.

When I was in my early twenties, he and I developed a holiday ritual of going to the hotel bar in the evening, before Mum and Jack would show up for dinner. We'd sink a cocktail or two and chat. Memory is an unreliable thing, but when I think back on these scenes with Dad, 'The Girl from Ipanema' is always playing somewhere in the background. Whenever I hear that song, I always think of Dad in a hotel bar, a Campari and soda in his hand, watching the sunset.

I treasure memories of my dad on holiday. Once, on a trip

to Crete when Jack and I were twelve and fourteen respectively, we wanted to go on the inflatable-tyre inner tubes – the ones that look like rubber doughnuts and are pulled along behind a speedboat. We were both strong swimmers – there would have been no need to have an adult accompany us – but Dad was having none of it. He strapped on a life jacket and arranged himself in the floating ring, his stout, hairy legs poking out at an acute angle. Unfortunately for him, as we sped along a wave flipped him up in the air and he lost his grip on the doughnut. He executed a perfect cartwheel mid-air and bellyflopped into the sea. Jack and I fell out of our rings too, helpless with laughter.

We are taking a late flight home. I was sick on the car journey to the airport so now I'm feeling tired and uncomfortable. I'm ambushed by a shot of grief. I prepared myself for the first trip without him; I didn't expect going home to a London without him to be the most painful bit. I gaze out of the aeroplane window.

It's a clear night and the awning of stars dwarfs the septic light pollution from the ground. Looking at the stars, I ask Dad if he's there. 'Yes, love, I'm here,' his voice answers.

Since he died, I often find myself saying 'Hello, Dad'. His cheerful gravelly tones pop into my mind, clear as a bell:

'Hello, love.' I ask him questions and tell him I love him; the answering voice is helpful and affectionate.

I don't fool myself into thinking that the voice of my dad is communicating with me from a spiritual plane. I know it's a manifestation of my grief. My brain is just doing its utmost to comfort me in my emotional destitution.

On the plane, I feel I need more proof than the voice's simple reassurance. 'Send me a sign, Dad,' I whisper. 'If you're listening, send me a sign.'

A shooting star blazes across the sky. Tears spill down my cheeks. I wish upon all the stars that I still possessed the wide-eyed, Disney naivety to believe in signs, angels or heaven. But that part of me died long ago.

The shooting star isn't Dad's soul sending me a message of solace. It's a speck of space dust hitting the earth's atmosphere at high velocity, creating heat and light in the process. I hope for another: perhaps two will convince me? Or three? A whole meteor shower? I press my face to the little plastic window, cupping my hands around my eyes.

Nothing happens. I'm not convinced. It was just a coincidence – my vulnerable mind is clutching at straws. The window steams up from the heat of my tears.

'Courage, dear heart,' says the voice.

'What?'

I wonder why I talk to someone who isn't there. I know full

well that it's just me, answering my own questions. Like a simple-minded budgie, hopping about its cage with a mirror, strategically hung to fool the poor beast into thinking it has a friend. But unlike the budgie, I know that the face in the mirror is my own.

'Have courage, dear heart,' says the voice. 'And stop crying. You've got snot dribbling down your nose.'

By now I'm sobbing openly. Other EasyJetters and cabin crew look at me with vague, bleary-eyed concern and insipid curiosity. Crying in public is mortifying in the extreme, but somehow it's exponentially worse with EasyJet.

I swab the snot and tears with my silk scarf – the same one I was wearing when he died. I soiled it with sadness then too, but I haven't sent it to the dry cleaner's, just in case there's a tiny scrap of him left on it.

'Get that scarf cleaned, for Gawd's sake. It looks like it's been on the floor of a pub khazi.'

EPILOGUE

THE FIRST ANNIVERSARY OF Dad's death rolls around quickly. The days have felt long but the year has passed by in a flash. Once again Mum, Jack and I take the now-familiar pilgrimage to his grave. Spring is in full flow. The place is covered with tentative new flowers, and the trees are lined with young leaves. The birds are singing their little hearts out. Dad died at a cheerful time of year – his last act of generosity. As I look at the gravestone, decorated with my oak-leaf design, I weep. There's no one but us around, and even if there were I wouldn't care. God, I miss him so much.

Over the next few days I notice something has shifted. His absence is still painful, but I'm learning to accept it. With every day I edge closer to being at peace. One night, before I drift off to sleep, I have the now-routine conversation in my head:

'Hi, Dad. I love you. I miss you.'

'Hello, love. I love you too, but I'm still with you, you know.'

Without warning, I have an irrefutable feeling: he is in heaven. I still don't actually believe in heaven or an afterlife, but this feeling transcends intellectual ideas. I suppose that's why they call it faith. He seems further away, but in a calm, warm place where he'll be at peace for eternity. I don't envisage him in a white gown with a halo, wings and a harp. Although an image of Bob the hairy-shouldered angel does amuse me, as it would him.

He was flawed, like everyone, but he was a good man and he deserves to be in heaven. Perhaps this is my mind's way of letting him go, or of putting his memory somewhere that feels tolerable. Either way, I am comforted.

I often look back over the '11 Lessons'. I don't always manage to follow Dad's words of advice. But they've become my template for living. If ever I find myself at a crossroads I'll return to them. It's the nearest I can get to asking him for advice.

As time heals the loss, I notice that my love for Dad has deepened. The process of writing this book has revealed a wealth of wonderful things about him that I never would have known otherwise. There were no great surprises: Dad was always consistent. But with every interview and new perspective, I gained deeper insight and my affection grew.

Along the way, people I talked to about Dad shared their

own stories of grief and loss. It reminds me that what my family has been through is universal.

Life is inherently tragic, because the only thing that is worth a damn in this transient world is love, and when we love we're vulnerable to loss. Grief is the price of love, and I would rather pay the toll than not love at all. Making friends with the sadness of life makes the journey considerably easier. I try to emulate Dad, accept what is and enjoy the moment, because any day it might be stolen. Love does not wither and die with the fallible human body. It pulls up an easy chair, settles down and makes itself good and comfortable in the heart. Dad may be gone, but our love endures.

ACKNOWLEDGEMENTS

I DOCUMENTED MY JOURNEY of grief with the help and support of my mother, who was herself mourning the loss of her soulmate. She was ready with compassion and cups of tea and she shouldered my burden along with her own. Mum always believed in me, even when my confidence faltered. Thank you, Mum.

Writing is a solitary job and tapping away at a keyboard long into the night can leave one feeling pretty isolated. However, I'm lucky enough to have never been alone. Collaborating with my brilliant, original, fearless co-author, Richard Butchins, was vital. He supported me through the highs and lows, was my mentor and my best friend. This book would not exist without him and I'm eternally grateful.

Huge thanks go to my husband Peter, who is a constant source of kindness and patience. He kept me grounded throughout the writing process.

Acknowledgements

The story of my relationship with my dad is personal and unique to me and I make no apologies for any bias on my part. However, I have three other siblings, Alex, Sarah and Jack, who have their own memories of Dad, and those recollections belong to them. I thank my siblings for supporting this project from the start.

I would like to thank my agent, Robert Kirby, who went above and beyond the call of duty to make this book happen. Robert was always on hand to offer sensible, informed guidance and kept the project on track.

I'd also like to thank the raft of contributors whose input was invaluable. During every interview I laughed like a drain and became privy to anecdotes I would never have known otherwise. Although I haven't used material from every interview, each one shed light on Dad's life and explained the man he became. Meeting his friends and colleagues and hearing their memories of him was fun, elucidating and moving. Thanks go to Kenneth Cranham, Dame Judi Dench, Dexter Fletcher, Stephen Frears, Gawn Grainger, Piers Haggard, Barry Hanson, James Hart, Norma Heyman, Dave Hill, Jane Wood, Sally Hope, Tamora Lee, Sylvester McCoy, Max von Massenbach, Zoë Nathenson, Sammy Pasha, Monique Perez, Jean Que, Fred Specktor, Cathy Tyson, Zoë Wanamaker, Ray Ward, Jaime Winstone, Ray Winstone, Steve Woolley and Robert Zemeckis. Thank you, everyone.